Business
and Industry

EDITORS

William R. Childs

Scott B. Martin

Wanda Stitt-Gohdes

VOLUME 6

INVENTORY to
MERRILL LYNCH

MARSHALL CAVENDISH

NEW YORK · TORONTO · LONDON · SYDNEY

Marshall Cavendish
99 White Plains Road
Tarrytown, New York 10591-9001

www.marshallcavendish.com

Library of Congress Cataloging-in-Publication Data

Business and industry / editors, William R. Childs, Scott B. Martin, Wanda Stitt-Gohdes.
        p. cm.
    Includes bibliographical reference and index.
    Contents: v. 1. Accounting and Bookkeeping to Burnett, Leo--v. 2. Business Cycles to Copyright--
v. 3. Corporate Governance to Entrepreneurship--v. 4. Environmentalism to Graham,
Katharine--v.5. Great Depression to Internship--v. 6. Inventory to Merrill Lynch--
v. 7. Microeconomics to Philip Morris Companies--v. 8. Price Controls to Sarnoff, David--
v. 9. Savings and Investment Options to Telecommuting--v. 10. Temporary Workers to Yamaha--
v. 11. Index volume
    ISBN 0-7614-7430-7 (set)--ISBN 0-7614-7436-6 (v. 6)
    1. Business--Encyclopedias. 2. Industries--Encyclopedias. I. Childs, William R., 1951-II. Martin,
Scott B., 1961-III. Stitt-Gohdes, Wanda.

HF1001 .B796 2003
338'.003--dc21   2002035156

Printed in Italy

06 05 04 03 5 4 3 2 1

MARSHALL CAVENDISH
Editorial Director   Paul Bernabeo
Production Manager   Alan Tsai

Produced by The Moschovitis Group, Inc.

THE MOSCHOVITIS GROUP
President, Publishing Division   Valerie Tomaselli
Executive Editor   Hilary W. Poole
Associate Editor   Sonja Matanovic
Design and Layout   Annemarie Redmond
Illustrator   Richard Garratt
Assistant Illustrator   Zahiyya Abdul-Karim
Photo Research   Gillian Speeth
Production Associates   K. Nura Abdul-Karim, Rashida Allen
Editorial Assistants   Christina Campbell, Nicole Cohen, Jessica Rosin
Copyediting   Carole Campbell
Proofreading   Paul Scaramazza
Indexing   AEIOU, Inc.

Alphabetical Table of Contents

Inventory

Inventory is a term for goods that are held by a business for sale or for use in production. The goods can be raw materials or parts used by manufacturers to produce finished goods. They can also be the finished goods themselves, which are held by manufacturers until they are sold to wholesalers, then held by wholesalers until they are sold to retailers, then held by retailers until they are sold to the public.

Although inventory is a simple idea, managing inventory can be very complicated. Stores often stock hundreds or thousands of different items, all of which need to be tracked and accounted for. A manufacturer might have inventories of hundreds of parts and dozens of different finished products.

Having too much or too little inventory can cause problems for a company. Too much inventory is quite expensive; the inventory must be stored, so space must be bought or rented and outfitted with security staff, light, and, depending upon the kind of inventory, refrigeration or other climate control. The longer inventory sits, the higher the risk that it will be damaged, stolen, become obsolete, or otherwise become worthless.

In addition, too much of inventory can represent a serious opportunity cost, which is the price of making one choice as opposed to another. For example, if a furniture wholesaler buys $10,000 worth of chairs, that $10,000 is lost to the wholesaler until the chairs are sold. If the chairs do not sell, the wholesaler's money remains tied up in inventory and cannot be used for anything else. Having too little inventory, however, is also a problem. If a manufacturer cannot produce a product in a timely fashion because she keeps running out of the necessary parts, her clients will buy the product from someone else.

Too little inventory also creates missed opportunities. In June 2001, for example, the singer Alicia Keys released her first album, *Songs in A Minor*. Sales of music had been slow that year, and Keys was unproven, so retailers refused to carry a large stock of her album. The album was a hit when it was released, and retailers quickly ran out of copies to sell. While some disappointed fans probably bought *Songs in A Minor* later, others probably never bought the album, limiting the profits of music retailers, the singer, and the album's producer.

The first step in properly managing inventory is to determine how much a company has on hand. One method is to look at how many goods a company had, for instance, at the beginning of the year, determine how many new goods were ordered during the year, and then see how many were sold or used during the year. This method assumes that those numbers are accurate and

See also:
Bar Code; Just-in-Time Inventory; Opportunity Cost; Supply and Demand.

Stacks of lumber in a hardware store. Stores must carry inventory so products are available when customers want to buy them.

that nothing else happened to the inventory—no theft, no breakage, no loss.

Companies generally want a more accurate inventory count. Before the widespread use of computers, most companies periodically "took inventory," often closing operations to count the number of units of the various goods held in inventory. This method lets a company know how much of a particular good is left; however, it is time-consuming and disrupts operations. Companies usually took inventory once or twice a year; for the rest of the year, exact inventory levels were unknown.

Computers have made so-called perpetual inventory—once reserved for companies that sold only a few very expensive goods—accessible to most businesses. By using bar codes and scanners, a grocery store can determine at any time how much of which products are being sold. This means that if a new cereal is wildly popular, the store's management knows immediately and is able to order more. The managers can even put up a special display of the cereal and find out whether that leads to more sales. Even with perpetual inventory, however, most stores find that occasionally taking inventory the old-fashioned way is useful to determine theft and breakage.

Computerized inventory systems can be networked to each other, which helped give rise to just-in-time inventory systems in the 1990s, an idea originally developed in Japan. Just-in-time inventory especially influenced manufacturers of complex machinery requiring lots of parts and supplies. In a perfect just-in-time inventory system, inventory all but disappears because networked inventory systems enable the supplier to provide the manufacturer with what she needs just when she needs it. In the real world, just-in-time systems tend to shift inventory costs from manufacturers to suppliers; however, such systems often result in less inventory overall.

This reduction appears to have benefited the U.S. economy. Usually when an economic recession or depression begins, manufacturers do not realize immediately that demand has slowed. (Manufacturers respond with layoffs or temporarily shutting plants and production lines.) During the lag time, inventories often build up just as demand has slacked, resulting in a large inventory "overhang." Because manufacturers have so much excess inventory sitting around (which costs money to store), they suddenly slow down production, selling goods out of inventory instead of manufacturing new goods. If enough manufacturers are affected, unemployment can suddenly increase, worsening the downturn.

Turnover Analysis

A turnover analysis helps decide if the investment in an individual inventory item is too low, too high, or just right. For example, this turnover analysis from a publishing company looks at the inventory of particular book titles.

Fall Publishing List				
Title	Number of units in stock	Number of units sold in last 30 days	Days until title is out of stock	Action
American First Ladies	2,500	357	210	None
Animals A-Z	750	250	90	Reprint title (increase inventory)
Astronomy Firsts	4,000	400	300	None
Cartoons for Everyone	10,000	35	8,571	Remainder 5,000 units (decrease inventory)
Geography of Afghanistan	1,300	856	45	Reprint title (increase inventory)

Computerized inventory systems enable companies to analyze up-to-the-minute data on the status of inventory.

In 2000, after many companies had adopted just-in-time inventory systems, an economic slowdown began. Initially, the slowdown demonstrated the limits of such systems; high-tech companies like Sun Microsystems were caught unawares by the slowdown, did not decrease production in time, and had massive inventory overhangs. However, the slowdown proved to be relatively mild, in part because manufacturers in general had relatively little excess inventory. The shallowness of the recession was attributable to a number of other factors as well, including consumer demand falling only mildly, so inventories cleared out faster. Nonetheless, the pace with which the U.S. economy recovered in 2001 did raise the possibility that advances in inventory management could result in less economic volatility in the future.

Further Reading

Hall, Robert W. *Zero Inventories.* Homewood, Ill.: Dow Jones-Irwin, 1983.

Plossl, George W. *Production and Inventory Control: Principles and Techniques.* 2nd ed. Englewood Cliffs, N.J.: Prentice-Hall, 1985.

Tersine, Richard J. *Principles of Inventory and Materials Management.* 3rd ed. New York: North-Holland, 1988.

Trent, Robert J. "Managing Inventory Investment Effectively." *Supply Chain Management Review,* 1 March 2002, 28.

Young, Jan B. *Modern Inventory Operations: Methods for Accuracy and Productivity.* New York: Van Nostrand Reinhold, 1991.

—*Mary Sisson*

Investment

Investment entails risking money in a venture to make more money. Ways one might invest are almost limitless. Whatever the form, the practice of investment involves weighing risk against return.

The Evolution of Investment Theory

Investing is probably nearly as old as the invention of money, which is ancient indeed. One well-known example is Jesus' parable in the New Testament (Luke 19:12–27), wherein the unsuccessful servant is chided, "Why then did you not put my money into the bank, and at my coming I should have collected it with interest?" The *Oxford English Dictionary* traces the English term *invest* (in the economic sense) to the early fourteenth century.

The scientific study of investment probability may be said to have begun in the 1650s, when the French philosopher Blaise Pascal laid down the foundations of probability theory. Some 40 years later, the

English astronomer Edmund Halley turned his attention to life tables, assessing the probabilities of life expectancies—a development that paved the way for the life insurance industry, and, eventually, other forms of insurance, the founding of Lloyd's of London, and the application of probability theory to the operation of the stock market.

In 1830 Justice Samuel Putnam of Massachusetts established the legal foundation for professional investment management with his so-called Prudent Man Rule: "Those with the responsibility to invest money for others should act with prudence, discretion, intelligence, and regard for the safety of capital as well as for income." In 1900 Louis Bachelier elaborated his Random Walk Theory, which held that stock prices change unpredictably as a result of unexpected information appearing in the market; his ideas were neglected until they were rediscovered in the 1960s and have been considerably refined.

A final milestone on the road to modern investment analysis is the development

An original stock certificate from the Ford Motor Company, issued to Henry Ford in 1903.

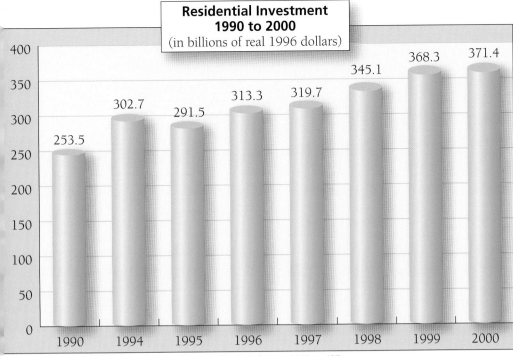

**Residential Investment
1990 to 2000**
(in billions of real 1996 dollars)

Year	Value
1990	253.5
1994	302.7
1995	291.5
1996	313.3
1997	319.7
1998	345.1
1999	368.3
2000	371.4

Source: U.S. Bureau of the Census, *Statistical Abstract of the United States,* 2001, p. 497.

of Modern Portfolio Theory by the economist Harry Markowitz in 1952. Markowitz weighted various risks of investing and demonstrated that an investor's risk can be reduced by balancing the expected return on the portfolio and its variance, or standard deviation. Many refinements of Bachelier and Markowitz's ideas have been made, and business libraries are full of books that strive to explain the secrets of successful investing.

Kinds of Investment

In general, investment is divided into two categories, personal and corporate—or, to use terms sometimes preferred by economists, financial investment (basically, the purchase of pieces of paper that earn interest) and capital investment (acquiring productive assets that can be used to produce goods and services; also called real investment). Bachelier and Markowitz's theories relate mostly to financial investment. A secure investment, for example, a savings account, usually pays a low return, while a riskier investment may bring great returns but also may be entirely lost. Financial or personal investments can turn into real investments. If, for example, money is deposited in a bank (financial investment), that bank may, in turn, lend that money to a business owner who uses it to buy machinery (real, or capital, investment).

Economists analyze real (or capital) investment. To an economist, investment means the purchase of capital assets: new structures, equipment, and inventory. Although spending money on anything that increases productivity qualifies as investment, in practice the U.S. government keeps data on three kinds of investment: business fixed investment (such items as buildings and equipment), business inventories, and residential investment.

Investment is one of the more volatile factors in a national economy, commonly rising or falling much more quickly or to a greater degree than the gross national product (GNP). Investment decisions require a long time to plan and implement, and the results of those decisions are long-lasting. For example, a builder may plan to construct a new office tower during a time in which office space is in great demand. By the time that building is erected, however, the nation might be in a recession, with the demand for office space declining. During the recession, office construction ceases

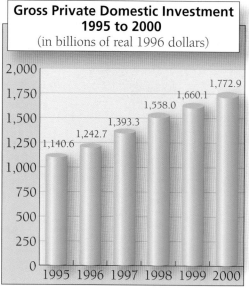

**Gross Private Domestic Investment
1995 to 2000**
(in billions of real 1996 dollars)

Year	Value
1995	1,140.6
1996	1,242.7
1997	1,393.3
1998	1,558.0
1999	1,660.1
2000	1,772.9

Source: U.S. Bureau of the Census, *Statistical Abstract of the United States*, 2001, p. 497.

(investment declines), which leads to a shortage of office space when conditions improve.

Analyzing Investment

A business's decision to invest depends on several factors. A business weighs the cost of investing against the amount of product or service it anticipates that it can sell as a result. Economists use the term *business confidence* to describe the mood in which a firm weighs its prospects, and the term *investment demand* to describe the amount that businesses desire to spend on new goods. Actual investment may be more or less than investment demand, depending on whether inventories are accumulating or being sold at an unexpectedly quick rate. Other factors that a business must consider include the prices of the assets it seeks to acquire, interest rates, and the taxes that will have to be paid when profits rise as a result of investment.

In the 1960s the economist Dale Jorgensen coined the phrase "user cost of capital" to describe the cumulative effects of the cost factors that make up an investment. Economists also point out that liquidity (a company's liquid assets, along with its current cash flow) is an important independent factor in investing—especially true for smaller businesses with cyclical cash flow, because these firms depend primarily on their internal funds to make investments.

As businesses compare the costs of capital investment with the revenues they expect to gain as a result, the percentage by which revenues exceed the cost of investment is known as the rate of return. Because companies normally contemplate making more than one investment at a time, they must rank their investment prospects by comparing the expected rates of return of those investments. As a rule, a good investment is one that earns a rate of return with a percentage that is higher than the market rate of interest—the rate of return on the investment should be higher than the rate of return from simply saving the money.

Economists use the same calculation to examine investment patterns in a national economy. As investments should be made when the expected rate of return exceeds the interest rate, the market rate of interest determines when investments occur (or when they do not). Wall Street is so concerned with the activities of the Federal

Examples of Personal Investing

- Savings accounts
- Certificates of deposit (CDs)
- Whole life insurance
- Treasury bills (T-bills)
- Commercial paper (unsecured short-term debt of various kinds of companies)

- Savings bonds and municipal bonds
- Equity investments (preferred and common stock)
- Mutual funds
- 401(k) plans
- Real estate
- Collectibles (coins, stamps, art, and so on)

Federal Reserve Board chairman Alan Greenspan testifies before the U.S. Congress Joint Economic Committee in June 1999. Investors closely monitor the decisions of the Fed because the Fed controls interest rates, which have a major impact on investments.

Reserve because the Federal Reserve sets the interest rate and therefore has a key role in the level of investment. Investment is inversely related to the interest rate—lower interest rates usually result in greater investment and higher interest rates usually result in lower investment. This pattern, known as the investment–demand curve, shifts in line with business confidence—the level of investment at a particular rate of interest can be higher or lower according to investors' evaluations of the economy's prospects.

Sometimes companies disinvest, or reduce their capital goods. If, for example, a company finds that it cannot sustain higher costs of operation, it may decide to sell some of its durable assets. Assuming that another company purchases these assets, capital goods in the nation as a whole do not decline. The term *disinvestment*, however, also refers to a decline in the total stock of capital goods in a national economy. This happens when the economy is not entirely replacing the assets that wear out or the inventory that is depleted (negative net investment). Such decline has not occurred in the United States since the Great Depression of the 1930s, although inventories have declined during periods of recession.

Further Reading

Bernstein, Peter L. *Against the Gods: The Remarkable Story of Risk.* New York: John Wiley & Sons, 1996.

Chancellor, Edward. *Devil Take the Hindmost: A History of Financial Speculation.* New York: Dutton/Plume, 2000.

Coase, Ronald H. *The Firm, the Market, and the Law.* Chicago: University of Chicago Press, 1990.

Grinblatt, Mark, and Sheridan Titman. *Financial Markets and Corporate Strategy.* 2nd ed. New York: McGraw-Hill/Irwin, 2002.

Jones, Charles P. *Investments: Analysis and Management.* 7th ed. New York: John Wiley & Sons, 2000.

Murphy, Austin. *Scientific Investment Analysis.* Westport, Conn.: Quorum Books, 2000.

Spaulding, David. *Measuring Investment Performance: Calculating and Evaluating Investment Risk and Return.* New York: McGraw-Hill, 1997.

—*Joseph Gustaitis*

Web Resources on Investing

www.investorwords.com is a comprehensive glossary of terms and concepts relating to financial investments.

www.aimr.com, home page of the Association for Investment Management and Research, which is an international, nonprofit organization of investment consultants and educators.

www.household.com/corp/hi_ca_financial_investment.jsp provides resources and advice for investors.

www.socialinvest.org provides resource guides and advice for socially responsible investing.

www.investment.com is a Canadian Web site that provides links and access to resources about all kinds of investments.

See also:

Globalization;
Interchangeable Parts;
International Trade; Total
Quality Management.

ISO 9000

ISO 9000 refers to 13 documents that lay out standards for the assessment of quality-management systems in business. The standards address the processes a business can follow to ensure that whatever it produces—from machine parts to administrative services—will be likely to meet a customer's requirements.

All businesses must satisfy their customers to survive. In business, therefore, quality is commonly assessed according to how well a product or service satisfies a customer's requirements. Since the 1970s, quality management and information related to it have become major concerns of businesses of all sizes, no matter where they manufacture and sell their products. Customers benefit from access to reliable information about suppliers' quality-management systems; suppliers benefit, too, as a supplier with many customers saves money, time, and effort by having its quality-management system checked early on, not merely by each customer after sales are made.

In this context, experts in quality management from around the world began working in 1979 to write the ISO 9000 standards. The first editions of the standards were published in 1987; the second, in 2000. They were developed within the International Organization for Standardization (ISO), an organization that creates technical specifications for a wide range of products, from nuts and bolts to medical equipment. The ISO also has crafted other agreements, including the protocols that allow people to withdraw money from their bank account in France using an automated teller machine (ATM) in the United States. Intended to expedite global trade in products and services, the ISO 9000 standards enable impartial, outside evaluators to audit a company's quality-management system. A system that is found to meet ISO 9000 standards is then registered or certified in a listing that is recognized worldwide.

According to ISO 9000 standards, quality management can be described by reference to eight key principles:

1. a business's focus on the customer;
2. the commitment of an organization's leadership;
3. the involvement of people in the system;
4. a process approach to quality management;
5. a systems approach to management;
6. a focus on continual improvement;
7. a factual approach to decision making; and
8. mutually beneficial supplier–customer relationships.

To the extent that organizations adhere to these principles, their quality-management systems are likely to satisfy customers. The particular means used to realize the

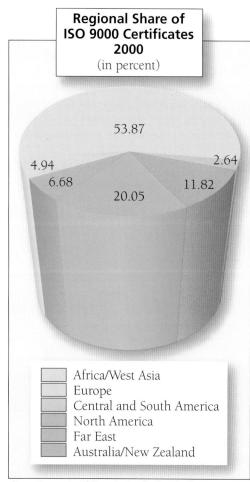

**Regional Share of
ISO 9000 Certificates
2000**
(in percent)

53.87

4.94   2.64

6.68   11.82

20.05

- [ ] Africa/West Asia
- [ ] Europe
- [ ] Central and South America
- [ ] North America
- [ ] Far East
- [ ] Australia/New Zealand

Source: International Organization for Standardization,
The ISO Survey of ISO 9000 and ISO 14000 Certificates,
10th cycle, http://www.isoeasy.org/survey10thcycle.pdf
(February 12, 2003).

The following documents compose the ISO 9000 series.

- ISO 9000: Fundamentals and terminology
- ISO 9004: Guidelines for performance improvements
- ISO 19011: Guidelines for auditing
- ISO 10005: Quality plan guidelines
- ISO 10006: Quality guidelines in project management
- ISO 10007: Guidelines for ensuring that a complex product, like some software programs, continues to function when parts are changed
- ISO 10012-1: Calibration system for measuring equipment
- ISO 10012-2: Guidelines for control of measurement of processes
- ISO 10013: Guidelines for developing quality manuals
- ISO/TR: Technical Report 10014: Guidelines for achieving economic benefits from quality management
- ISO 10015: Quality training guidelines
- ISO/TS 16949: Particular quality-management system requirements for automotive suppliers

principles, of course, will affect the actual level of quality attained for any particular product or service.

The key standard in the ISO 9000 series is ISO 9001, which lays down the actual requirements for a quality-management system. An organization independent of the supplier and its customers evaluates the supplier's quality-management system to determine whether it meets the ISO 9001 requirements. The independent organization is often a testing laboratory. Businesses seeking ISO 9000 certification can check to see whether a potential evaluator (also called an auditor) has been accredited by a national organization and found to be competent. When a business is found to have met the applicable requirements, the auditor certifies its quality-management system as in compliance with ISO 9001. The business can then share this information with its current and potential customers.

Some industries have used the ISO 9000 standards as a base and added industry-specific requirements for their suppliers to meet. Auto manufacturers have done so with QS 9000 (in North America) and ISO/TS (Technical Specification) 16949.

ISO 9000 standards are comprehensive in scope, covering topics that range from technical terminology to management, training, and (in some cases) industry-specific guidelines. Taken together, these standards can provide guidance for companies seeking to develop and improve their quality-management systems.

In an example of how ISO might be used, the key customers of a chemical processing company required that its quality-management system be certified to ISO 9001 (quality-management system requirements). The company decided to use ISO 9000 (fundamentals and terminology) and ISO 9004 (guidelines for performance improvements) to develop a complete quality-management strategy. As a result, the company found that it should apply all elements of ISO 9001 when having its quality-management system audited. The company then applied ISO 10013 (guidelines for developing quality manuals) to develop its quality documentation and ISO 10015 (quality training guidelines) to put appropriate employee-training programs in place.

Another example of ISO in action involves growth. A developer of software

Growth of ISO Certifications Worldwide 1995 to 2000

	1995	1996	1997	1998	1999	2000
Africa/West Asia	3,378	6,162	8,668	12,150	17,307	20,185
Share in percent	2.26	3.79	3.88	4.47	5.04	4.94
No. of countries	27	37	40	48	49	52
Central and South America	1,220	1,713	2,989	5,221	8,972	10,805
Share in percent	0.96	1.05	1.34	1.92	2.61	2.64
No. of countries	15	19	23	28	29	30
North America	10,374	16,980	25,144	33,550	45,166	48,296
Share in percent	8.15	10.44	11.25	12.34	13.14	11.82
No. of countries	3	3	3	3	3	3
Europe	92,611	109,961	143,674	166,255	190,248	220,127
Share in percent	72.72	67.58	64.31	61.13	55.36	53.87
No. of countries	36	38	42	42	47	50
Far East	9,240	18,407	29,878	37,920	56,648	81,919
Share in percent	7.26	11.31	13.42	13.99	16.48	20.05
No. of countries	13	14	16	18	20	21
Australia/New Zealand	10,526	9,478	12,946	16,751	25,302	27,299
Share in percent	8.27	5.83	5.79	6.16	7.36	6.68
No. of countries	2	2	2	2	2	2

Source: International Organization for Standardization, The ISO Survey of ISO 9000 and ISO 14000 Certificates, 10th cycle, http://www.isoeasy.org/survey10thcycle.pdf (February 12, 2003).

for a specific application saw its user base expanding and recognized that it needed a strategy to manage the product as its configuration changed in response to changes in user requirements, operating systems, user hardware, and legal requirements. It used ISO 9004 to get guidance on establishing and documenting procedures to improve the necessary processes. It also found ISO 10006 and ISO 10007 helpful in managing the project itself and in preparing procedures for ensuring that the software would continue to function when parts of it were changed.

The ISO 9000 series of standards allows a business to tell customers that its quality-management system has been measured against globally accepted standards. Customers then can have more confidence that the products and services they buy will meet their needs. The standards provide a rational, economically efficient way to describe and improve quality-management systems and to communicate this information to customers around the world.

Nations with Largest Annual Growth in ISO 9000 Certification 2000

Number of certificates

China 10,548
Italy 9,298
Japan 6,765
South Korea 3,891
Spain 3,877
Czech Republic 2,955

Source: International Organization for Standardization, The ISO Survey of ISO 9000 and ISO 14000 Certificates, 10th cycle, http://www.isoeasy.org/survey10thcycle.pdf (February 12, 2003).

Further Reading

American Society for Quality. http//www.asq.org/stand/types/iso9000.html (February 13, 2003).
International Organization for Standardization. http//www.iso.ch/iso/en/iso9000–14000 (February 13, 2003).

—Karen Boehme

Job Search

A job search is not a once-in-a-lifetime opportunity. A worker typically is in the job market many times in his or her career. The basics of a job search—preparation, process, contact, and negotiation—are the same for the searcher just starting out or one close to retirement.

Preparation

The largest amount of time is usually put into the preparation phase. Preparation includes self-analysis for career direction, writing a resume, determining a target market or target company, and basic research on salary and benefits for the target market.

The first question to be answered is, "What do I want to do with my life?" Although it may take many years to find the answer, asking questions along those lines can help direct a job search. For example, do I like to work with people or things? Do I want a traditional job or something a little out of the ordinary? Am I willing to get additional education or

See also:
Compensation; Human Capital; Human Resources; Resume.

Newspapers usually feature a "Help Wanted" section that can be searched for jobs.

training to meet my goals? How much money do I need to be making in five years to live the way I desire without going into debt? The answers to these questions either open up areas or close them off during the job search. Fewer options are best when starting the task of creating a resume as a resume should be somewhat tailored to a specific job or industry.

A potential employer's first impression is typically taken from a resume. A resume should give the reviewer a fair idea of the person's experience and career goals or employment objective. When just starting out, a resume should be kept to one page. The key to a just-getting-started resume is to quantify everything possible. Quantifying experience adds value beyond the job description. For example, the job description for a food service job should go beyond flipping burgers and bussing tables. It should also say something like "learned

excellent communication skills through public contact." To quantify experience as a lifeguard, the resume could read, "ability to think clearly and act quickly in life-threatening situations" or "ability to remain calm in stressful situations, influencing others to stay calm." As early experience probably does not match career goals, these statements tell potential employers a tremendous amount about how the applicant interacts with others or functions in a work environment. Known as soft skills, they can be just as valuable as work experience.

Targeting a market further narrows the job search. A target helps job hunters clarify their objective in applying for particular jobs. A target also helps define how much they can expect to get paid for a job and where the career path will most likely lead in a few years.

Process

Once preparation is complete, the job search begins. A job search should be treated as a full-time job with office hours and appointment scheduling. The search can be an emotional roller coaster with highs and lows as interviews take place and offers may or may not be made. The key to keeping the emotions level and the number of interviews high is to keep sending out resumes and making contacts in a steady stream, even when a particular job seems promising. If the job falls through, valuable time has been lost if the search has stopped, and sometimes getting the momentum going again is difficult.

The most typical places to look for jobs are newspapers and the Internet. However, several other options are available. Networking with other people often produces good job matches for both the employer and job hunter because the personal referral works both ways. The person doing the referring usually knows a little about the company and a little about the person; that person has, in effect, done the first round of screening for the company. Bulletin boards at colleges and universities have job listings and internships. Another

Average Number of Jobs Held from Ages 18 to 34 1978 to 1998				
Sex and educational attainment	Number of jobs held by age			
	Total[1]	18 to 24 years old	25 to 29 years old	30 to 34 years old
Male				
Less than a high school diploma	10.7	6.1	3.5	2.8
High school graduates, no college	9.1	5.5	3.1	2.5
Less than a bachelor's degree	10.0	6.0	3.4	2.6
Bachelor's degree or more	9.3	6.0	2.9	2.4
Total	9.6	5.8	3.2	2.6
Female				
Less than a high school diploma	7.4	4.0	2.2	2.0
High school graduates, no college	8.2	4.8	2.5	2.3
Less than a bachelor's degree	9.2	5.6	3.0	2.4
Bachelor's degree or more	10.1	6.6	3.1	2.3
Total	8.8	5.4	2.8	2.3
Both sexes				
Less than a high school diploma	9.3	5.2	3.0	2.4
High school graduates, no college	8.7	5.2	2.8	2.4
Less than a bachelor's degree	9.6	5.8	3.2	2.5
Bachelor's degree or more	9.7	6.3	3.0	2.4
Total	9.2	5.6	3.0	2.4

[1] Jobs held in more than one age category were counted in each category, but only once in the total.
Source: U.S. Bureau of Labor Statistics, *Number of Jobs Held, Labor Market Activity, and Earnings Growth Over Two Decades: Results from a Longitudinal Survey,* USDL 00-119, Washington, D.C., Government Printing Office, 2000.

Search method	1994	1995	1996	1997	1998	1999
Contacted employer directly	67.4	65.1	64.7	67.3	64.5	65.1
Public employment agency	20.4	20.1	18.9	19.1	20.4	15.9
Private employment agency	7.2	7.1	7.5	6.6	6.6	7.0
Friends or relatives	15.7	18.0	16.6	14.6	13.5	13.4
School employment center	2.3	1.9	2.3	2.7	2.3	1.6
Sent out resumes/filled out applications	40.2	46.9	48.3	46.6	48.3	47.6
Checked union/professional registers	2.7	2.4	2.5	1.7	1.5	1.9
Placed or answered ads	16.7	17.7	17.3	16.3	14.5	12.5
Other active search methods	3.5	2.9	3.9	4.6	4.4	5.7

Methods of Job Searching 1994 to 1999 (in percent)

Note: Civilian noninstitutionalized population 16 and over who are unemployed active job seekers; based on the *Current Population Survey.*
Source: U.S. Bureau of Labor Statistics, *Monthly Labor Review,* October 2000.

method is to list companies that fit certain criteria and contact them directly.

Contact

An employer typically requires one or more interviews before making a hiring decision. A series of interviews might include an initial phone interview, then a personal interview with the hiring manager, then a team interview with peers. Each of these interviews serves a different purpose. The phone interview gives the employer basic information: How does the applicant handle himself over the phone? It also allows the employer to verify that the resume is true on a very basic level. The interview with the hiring manager gives the manager a feel for how the candidate's experience and personality will fit within the team dynamic and the corporate culture. The interview with peers serves two purposes. One is to verify hands-on experience at an in-depth level and the other is to see if the person is a fit for the company overall. Several interviews allow the company to evaluate experience plus soft skills, thus allowing the firm to make better hiring decisions.

An interview is a good time for the job hunter to find out some details about the company, too. For example, does the company offer any specific career paths? Does it have a mentoring program and who is eligible for it? What is the management structure like? Does the company pay for training as skills become outdated or new technology is developed? Another issue is the total benefits package. Often, this information is not available until after the company makes a job offer. Benefits can include various kinds of insurance, tuition reimbursement, telecommuting opportunities, flexible hours (flex time), overtime pay, retirement plans, and stock options.

The key to a good interview is preparation and confidence. Before the interview, research the company: check its Web site, check its reputation, know a little about its major products or services, and know what the company is looking for in new hires.

Questions about age, race, marital status, sexual orientation, number of children, or medical history are illegal. However, companies can, and often do, look up credit reports, which have information about litigation settlements, amount of debt, medical payment history to hospitals or doctors, and marital status. Some companies have requirements like drug testing before employment or the signing of non-compete agreements in which an employee agrees not to take a new job with a competing firm for a set amount of time. Job hunters should know the legal restraints on employers.

Although classified ads in newspapers are still a source for many jobs, increasingly people are finding jobs via the Internet.

Web Resources for Job Searches

www.monster.com is a comprehensive job search engine for both employers and candidates; it includes information on job openings, resumes, and interview guidelines.

www.dice.com provides employment resources for technology professionals.

www.careerbuilder.com posts employment opportunities for a variety of companies in many different fields.

www.fedworld.gov/jobs/jobsearch.html and www.federaljobsearch.com are Web sites listing employment opportunities with the federal government.

www.rileyguide.com is a guide to employment opportunities and job resources on the Internet.

www.provenresumes.com is a resource for helpful guides to resumes and cover letters.

www.job-hunt.org is a comprehensive list of the Web's best job search sites.

www.idealist.org is a resource for employment in the not-for-profit sector.

Once an interview is finished, a job seeker should follow up. Asking when a hiring decision will be made is appropriate; follow up with a phone call if the deadline passes. A thank you note for time spent with various interviewers lets the company know the applicant is serious and still interested. Follow-up is professional and it makes a big impression.

Negotiation

Subtle negotiation begins the minute the conversation turns to salary, compensation, or benefits. Every job hunter should be prepared to work through the salary negotiation process. Usually the negotiations begin awkwardly, with each party trying to have the other name a starting salary first. The job hunter can prepare by researching appropriate answers and practicing them beforehand. The salary figure is key because, in general, all future raises are based on the starting salary. Most employers work within a salary range for hiring based on demand for those skills, geographic location, and their own financial situation.

Salary is just one issue for negotiation. Benefits can sometimes be negotiated. Health insurance is usually not negotiable, but flex time, telecommuting, bonuses, number of vacation days, or relocation packages often can be negotiated. Negotiation in these areas primarily depends on demand. If the job market is soft or the skill set is readily available, then the employer has no need to negotiate over these items.

After negotiation, the final step is evaluating offers. As noted above, the offer is more than just a salary. It is a total compensation package. It must be reviewed in light of the job hunter's long- and short-term goals. For example, if the job is simply a stepping stone to another company, salary may be most important. If the plan is to stay a while, then family medical plans, matching funds for retirement packages, and telecommuting may weigh heavily in the decision to accept an offer. If a goal is to relocate, then paid relocation can have tremendous value.

The four phases of a job search—preparation, process, contact, and negotiation—can occur in a very condensed period, or they may take months. In many ways, a job search is a numbers game. The more potential employers that see a resume, the better the chances of getting a job. The keys to a successful job hunt are preparation and diligence in carrying out the search.

Further Reading

Bolles, Richard Nelson. *What Color is Your Parachute? 2003: A Practical Manual for Job Hunters and Career Changers.* Berkeley, Calif.: Ten Speed Press, 2002.

Damp, Dennis V. *The Book of U.S. Government Jobs: Where They Are, What's Available, and How to Get One.* 7th ed. New York: Brookhaven Press, 2000.

Engineering Your Job Search: A Job-Finding Resource for Engineering Professionals. Belmont, Calif.: Professional Publications, 1995.

Kennedy, Joyce Lain. *Job Interviews for Dummies.* 2nd ed. Foster City, Calif.: IDG Books Worldwide, 2000.

Rosenburg, Arthur D., and David V. Hizer. *The Resume Handbook: How to Write Outstanding Resumes and Cover Letters for Every Situation.* 3rd ed. Avon, Mass.: Adams Media, 1996.

Wood, Lamont. *Your 24/7 Online Job Search Guide.* New York: John Wiley & Sons, 2002.

—*Stephanie Buckwalter*

Johnson, John H.

1918–
Publisher

As founder of *Ebony* magazine and chairman of Johnson Publishing Company, John H. Johnson is one of America's most respected businessmen. An African American, Johnson has been credited with having a Midas touch, but he attributes his success to hard work and tenacity.

Johnson was born in 1918, the last year of World War I, in a tin-roofed house in Arkansas City, Arkansas. His father, a sawmill worker, died in an accident when Johnson was only eight. Despite poverty, Gertrude Johnson was determined to see her son get a good education. They moved to Chicago to find a black high school, and Johnson flourished there. He began writing for the school paper; as a senior, Johnson became editor in chief of the paper and sales manager for the school yearbook.

Johnson won a partial scholarship to the University of Chicago, but could not afford to attend full-time. He took a part-time job at Supreme Liberty Life Insurance Company. He was soon editor of the company's monthly newspaper, *The Guardian*, where he learned to allocate his time, follow up on details, and determine if activities advanced his interests.

At age 24, Johnson decided that the black community needed a publication targeted specifically to it, similar in style to *Life* and *Reader's Digest*. For two months he sought investment help from black businessmen, but none were willing to risk their money on him or his venture. Johnson then sought encouragement from Roy Wilkins, editor of *The Crisis*, the magazine of the National Association for the Advancement of Colored People (NAACP). Even Wilkins told him to drop the idea, arguing that he should spare himself disappointment—no one had ever published a successful black commercial magazine.

Unwilling to let his dream die, Johnson approached the First National Bank of Chicago for a loan. He was told the bank did not make loans to "colored people." However, a different bank, the Citizens Loan Corporation, was willing to lend him $500 if he could offer some collateral. Johnson's mother agreed to put up her new furniture, and Johnson put his plan into action.

Using the mailing list of the 20,000 Supreme Liberty Life Insurance Company customers, Johnson mailed $2 subscription offers. He hoped to entice the potential subscribers by giving them what they wanted: recognition and respect in a society that was still very much prejudiced against blacks. His strategy was built on an important sales principle: Ask not what you want, but what the customer wants. Three thousand people responded, sending in the $6,000 he needed to publish the first issue.

On November 1, 1942, *Negro Digest* rolled off the press; it was a pocket-sized publication that summarized newspaper and magazine articles about black life. With no staff, Johnson was the publisher, editor, business manager, and circulation manager; until 1944, he and his secretary were the company's only full-time employees. Circulation hovered around 50,000

See also:
Entrepreneurship;
Publishing Industry.

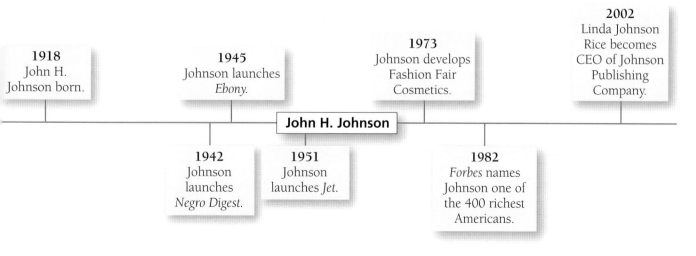

2002
Linda Johnson Rice becomes CEO of Johnson Publishing Company.

1918
John H. Johnson born.

1945
Johnson launches *Ebony*.

1973
Johnson develops Fashion Fair Cosmetics.

John H. Johnson

1942
Johnson launches *Negro Digest*.

1951
Johnson launches *Jet*.

1982
Forbes names Johnson one of the 400 richest Americans.

People are always telling me that I'm lucky, but luck is a word we use for an order that is not understood. I made some of my luck. I made it by working hard and trusting the logic of events, which always favor the bold and the active and the prepared.

There was another lesson that has served me well, and that is that history, money, and all the forces of the universe are on the side of the man or woman who sets a goal and works night and day to achieve it. That person may not win today. He may not win what he wants to win—which may not be, in the long sight of history, what he or she needs to win—but if he determines to work and will, he can't be denied.

—John H. Johnson, *Succeeding against the Odds*

until the first lady, Eleanor Roosevelt, penned an article for the magazine's regular feature, "If I Were a Negro." Circulation jumped to 100,000 and Johnson was able to expand his staff.

Johnson decided that blacks would also be interested in a glamorous photo magazine presenting, as he described it, "positive, everyday achievements from Harlem to Hollywood." In November 1945, the last year of World War II, Johnson's second magazine, *Ebony*, was born. Black professionals, entertainers, athletes, and others were presented as role models. The glossy magazine was expensive to produce. Juggling accounts to keep

Ebony afloat, Johnson spent more than a year securing his first white advertiser, Zenith Radio. Other advertisers followed. *Ebony* has remained the nation's number one black-oriented magazine for more than 50 years.

His third magazine, *Jet*, premiered in November 1951. The magazine's name represents Johnson's nod to the ever-increasing pace of society. *Jet* was designed to give blacks a quick weekly news update on everything from entertainment to sports to politics. Within six months, *Jet* had a circulation of 300,000, and it has remained a strong seller.

Johnson is credited with being an industry trailblazer; he influenced advertisers to market directly to African Americans and pushed for the use of models of color in advertising. This led to more opportunities for blacks in advertising, public relations, and modeling. Over the years Johnson has received numerous awards for his industry achievements and philanthropic efforts.

In 1973, at age 55, Johnson branched into the cosmetics industry. His *Ebony* models were having trouble finding makeup that matched their skin tones, and he was angered that cosmetics companies were not interested in creating a line for black women. Despite losing a million dollars a year for the first five years of development, Fashion Fair Cosmetics has become the most successful makeup and skin care company for women of color around the world.

In 1982 *Forbes* magazine listed Johnson as one of the 400 richest Americans. In 1984 the family-owned company became the top black-owned business in the country. In his eighties Johnson turned over most of the day-to-day operations to his daughter, Linda Johnson Rice, who became president and chief executive officer. Johnson Publishing Company is worth nearly $500 billion.

Further Reading

Falkof, Lucille. *John H. Johnson, "The Man from Ebony."* Ada, Okla.: Garrett Educational Corporation, 1992.
Johnson, John H. *Succeeding against the Odds.* New York: Warner Books, 1989.

—*Sheri Rehwold*

John Johnson and his daughter, Linda Johnson Rice, who is now president of the Johnson Publishing Company, in 1992.

Just-in-Time Inventory

Just-in-time (JIT) inventory management is not only a process or method of streamlining business and reducing inventory; rather, it is also a business philosophy that focuses on meeting customer requirements with 100 percent quality while eliminating waste. JIT is getting the right product to the right customer at the right time. It requires a combination of tools, techniques, and participation by people inside and outside the organization. The purpose of JIT is to lessen production cycle times and lower costs while increasing quality, which should, in turn, increase market share.

History of JIT

Tai-ichi Ohno of Japan is often considered the father of the concept. He worked for Toyota in the 1970s when Toyota's president said, essentially, that the car manufacturer had three years to catch up to U.S. automakers or face a total decline of the Japanese auto industry. Toyota did not use research and development as the catalyst for change. Instead, it imported technology from the West and focused on quality and reliability.

Ohno's challenge was to meet the Japanese domestic market demand and increase profits. The market required many different automobile models, but overall demand was fairly low. Low demand translated to a fixed selling price. As he could not increase the price of the vehicle, his only alternative was to lower the price of producing the vehicles. First, he looked at U.S. auto plants where workers were outproducing the Japanese at a rate of nine to one. He noted their use of economic order quantities—the practice of making a large batch of one item before retooling machines to make another. Because of the low demand for autos in Japan and the need to produce many different models, Ohno realized this kind of production would not work for Toyota. Instead, he based his system on the elimination of waste.

Ohno identified six areas of waste in the production process: (1) overproduction of goods, (2) waiting time along the production line, (3) transportation within the factory, (4) processing time for parts, (5) inventory held on site, and (6) product defects. Based on Ohno's analysis, Toyota made several changes to its operation, reconfiguring factory layout to reduce transportation and movement within the facility and reduce set-up time for retooling machines. It introduced product leveling— evening out the flow of production to meet product demand. For example, if the assembly of 40 components was required in one 40-hour workweek, then the factory would produce only one per hour. Leveling was extended to raw materials coming into the plant as well as the finished products shipped out, which helped reduce inventory on both sides of the equation.

One of the biggest changes was implementing the team concept—where the team included everyone along the production line. Ohno introduced the analogy of the team members as runners in a relay race where the baton is handed off from one runner to the next. If the baton is dropped (a problem encountered) anywhere along the way, production stops until the problem is fixed and the baton is ready to be passed. This method of running production was a drastic departure

See also:
Assembly Line;
Manufacturing Industry;
Productivity; Total Quality
Management; Wal-Mart.

Toyota employee Tai-ichi Ohno was the mind behind JIT.

from the hierarchical structure of managers and line workers, with quality inspectors on the side. It required that workers along the line inspect their product and fix problems as they arose. This method gave each worker responsibility for quality.

American Adaptation

JIT came into vogue in U.S. companies beginning in the 1980s. Foreign competition forced U.S. automakers to reevaluate themselves in terms of production, price, and quality. As competition increased and market share declined, U.S. automakers scrambled to make changes. Japanese imports were marginally more expensive, but they were of higher quality, requiring less maintenance in the long term. The U.S. automakers studied Japanese methods of production, which revolved around JIT. Implementing JIT principles helped General Motors jump ahead of rival Ford Motor Company as the number one car manufacturer in the United States for a time.

Many changes had to be made in U.S. manufacturing to accommodate the JIT

General Motors used JIT management to surpass Ford.

philosophy. First, the mentality that supported producing mass amounts of product, including many extra parts and components "just in case" they were needed, was abandoned. JIT requires just enough product at the right time to meet customer demand. Changing to "just enough product" meant producing smaller batches that could be moved along the supply chain to keep inventory stocks low, both in raw materials and end products. These smaller batches smoothed the flow of production by reducing wait time for retooling, problems, and inventory delivery.

Quality control processes also had to change. Manufacturers typically had quality inspectors along the line who would inspect products for defects. Because products were produced in large batches, many defective pieces might be made before the defect was found, making repair or replacement expensive both in time and money. This process gave management the final say on how to solve the problem and created a tendency to cover up problems as any downtime slowed production, which cost money. With JIT

manufacturing, everyone on the production line is responsible for the quality of what they produce. If problems are encountered anywhere along the line, production is shut down until a solution can be found. Although this stops production up and down the line, problems are found earlier and team members collaborate on the solution. Collaboration ensures that everyone up and down the line looks at the problem so a fix at one point does not create a problem at another point.

The culture and management structure of U.S. automobile companies did not support this kind of change and interaction. The typical manufacturing company before 1980 operated under the rule that management made all decisions and directed all the work. Authority was unquestioned. Line workers were measured on efficiencies and managers were measured on their ability to handle emergencies. By contrast, the keys to JIT are simplicity, flexibility, quality, and continuous improvement. Continuous improvement equals continuous change, which requires flexibility in both structure and attitude.

In 1982 Harley-Davidson implemented several changes in its U.S. operations, one of which was JIT. The motorcycle manufacturer had gone from a 70 percent market share in the 1950s to only 5.2 percent by 1981. The production line suffered from overstock of some parts with simultaneous shortages of others, as well as a large amount of waste. By 1985 Harley-Davidson had reduced defects by just over half and warranty claims by about one-third. By 1986 the company was thriving, in part because of JIT.

Some companies, Dell Computer among them, began using JIT principles as part of their corporate culture. Like Toyota in the early days, they did not rely on developing their own technology to win market share. Rather, they focused on building a superior supply chain process. They bucked the traditional business model of buying inventory, then holding it until it was sold; the Dell philosophy is "don't start building until you get an order." Dell based its business on the idea of selling a product, then building it and shipping it right away. This method requires

Just-in-Time Manufacturing vs. Traditional Manufacturing	
Just-in-Time Manufacturing	**Traditional Manufacturing**
Low or zero inventory	Large inventories built in anticipation of demand
Raw materials purchased and goods produced to order	Raw materials purchased and goods produced to forecast
Goods pulled through system by orders	Goods pushed through system by forecast
Management responsible for quality	Team members responsible for quality

discipline and a close working relationship with consistent, reliable suppliers.

Problems with JIT

A company considering adopting JIT must assess its competitive position and willingness to change. Competitors may already be too far ahead. Changing a company's culture and internal structure is not an overnight process. For example, Toyota needed 10 years of JIT before implementing a streamlined system of material flows through the company. Problems with delivery, design, or quality can take more time to fix than the market will allow. Employee morale can take a dive when workers who see inventory as a part of job security witness its evaporation. A different set of skills is involved when problems arise; JIT requires real problem solving to get to the root cause of a problem, as opposed to relying on quick fixes simply to keep the production line going.

Other aspects of JIT implementation can be potential problems. For example, JIT requires short set-up times to keep the line going; it demands a disciplined process from start to finish with no room for mistakes or late delivery. It also requires a stable demand to support level production. Finally, it requires cooperation and trust among team members and by management. Each of these is a potential point of failure when implementing a JIT system.

Changes in JIT

JIT is a relatively new concept in the business world. It can be implemented in a low-tech

Checkout lines at a Wal-Mart in Mexico City. JIT techniques originally conceived for manufacturing were applied by Wal-Mart in its hugely successful retail business.

environment, but it also benefits from high-tech solutions like those offered by the Internet. For example, e-commerce allows suppliers to keep real-time records of customer orders, allowing them to respond quickly and efficiently to changes in demand.

Many companies are also turning to Web-based communications. Information can be exchanged with suppliers without worrying about computer systems that cannot communicate. The supply chain becomes more efficient, resulting in lower transaction costs. Information can be exchanged in real time in much the same way that shipping companies use bar codes for tracking, which allows customers to check the status online. Software development in this area focuses on a comprehensive solution that addresses the communication between the company, suppliers, and the customer.

JIT in Nonmanufacturing Environments

Sam Walton began using JIT in Wal-Mart stores as early as the 1970s. Wal-Mart does not manufacture any products, but it uses JIT in its distribution of goods. Wal-Mart uses a networking system that links retail stores, redistribution centers, suppliers, and manufacturers. When a Wal-Mart store associate places an order, it is automatically sent to suppliers, redistribution centers, and the transportation companies. Item information can be tracked throughout the distribution chain. Wal-Mart's computer network is so essential to the success of the retailer's JIT distribution system that its

use is required for any company that wants to do business with Wal-Mart.

JIT has also produced several spin-offs Total Quality Management and the idea o "reinventing" a company to stay competitive The ideas that drive JIT in manufacturing car be applied to any industry or in any department of a company. For example, any proces in a company can be analyzed for waste and be made more efficient by using these same principles. The company or department can also constantly strive for 100 percent quality in al its dealings with its customers, whether those customers are internal or external to that company. Companies can restructure their organizational plans to be more flexible and mee changing market demands. The goal of these changes is the same in manufacturing or management: to produce a better product and increase profit. Any company can benefit from the JIT goal of continuous improvement.

Further Reading

Adair-Heeley, Charlene B. *The Human Side of Just-in Time: How to Make the Techniques Really Work.* New York: AMACOM, 1991.

Lowson, Bob, et al. *Quick Response: Managing the Supply Chain to Meet Consumer Demand.* New York: John Wiley and Sons, 1999.

Monden, Yasuhiro. *Toyota Production System: An Integrated Approach to Just-In-Time.* 3rd ed. Norcross, Ga.: Engineering and Management Press, 1998.

Ohno, Tai-ichi. *Toyota Production System: Beyond Large-scale Production.* Cambridge, Mass.: Productivity Press, 1988.

—*Stephanie Buckwalte*

Kellogg Company

Many people in the United States begin the day with a bowl of cereal. Hundreds of breakfast cereals on store shelves are loaded with sugar, and few people would consider them to be health foods. Ironically, the breakfast cereal industry was created by a man who wanted to give people something more nutritious to eat in the morning.

The Kellogg Company was founded by Will Keith Kellogg, but the story of the company really begins with his brother, Dr. John Harvey Kellogg. The Kelloggs were members of the Seventh-day Adventist Church, a Christian sect that requires strict dietary controls, including abstaining from meat and alcohol. Nineteenth-century Adventist leader Ellen G. White opened the Western Health Reform Institute in Battle Creek, Michigan, in 1866 to offer wealthy clients Adventist theology, health foods like oatmeal, and open-air exercise. Dr. Kellogg took over the failing institute in 1876.

Kellogg renamed the institute the Medical and Surgical Sanitarium (although it soon became known as the Battle Creek Sanitarium, or simply the "San"). For the next 60 years, the San would become Kellogg's laboratory for developing and promulgating his Battle Creek Idea—that good health and fitness were the result of good diet, exercise, correct posture, fresh air, and proper rest. Kellogg introduced a regime of treatments that was as bizarre as it was popular, and the rich and famous flocked to Battle Creek to try the latest health crazes. One of Kellogg's more unusual treatments involved a special diet for hypertension: up to 14 pounds of grapes per day and nothing else. Kellogg was also enamored of then-unheard-of health foods like yogurt, tofu, and gluten wafers.

Over the next few years Kellogg put many new items on the market, including granola and peanut butter. The products were given catchy names and Kellogg organized a new company to manufacture and market each one. Packaged in brightly colored boxes and easy to prepare, many of these foods were an instant success. Eventually, the growing popularity of his products led Dr. Kellogg to hire his younger brother Will as business manager.

Both Kelloggs were fascinated with creating a flaked breakfast cereal as a replacement for bread. John Kellogg later claimed the process came to him in a dream in 1890. The brothers boiled up some wheat, rolled it out into strips and baked it in the oven. The resulting cereal was a huge hit at the sanitarium, and the Kelloggs set up the Sanitas Nut Food Company, with Will as general manager, to sell the cereal by mail order to former sanitarium patients.

See also:
Genetic Engineering; Health Care Services Industry.

Dr. John Harvey Kellogg in 1937.

One former patient, C. W. Post, asked Dr. Kellogg's permission to license the cereal. When Kellogg refused, Post opened a factory of his own in Battle Creek, and marketed Grape Nuts and Post Toasties (originally called Elijah's Manna). Post became extremely wealthy as a craze for the new, cold breakfast cereal swept the nation. Cereal entrepreneurs flocked to Battle Creek to make their fortunes by inventing new cereals. By 1900 Battle Creek was nicknamed Cereal City, and at least 44 companies were churning out cereals with names like Per-Fo, Tryabita, and Orange Meat.

In 1906 Will finally convinced his brother to let him market the original breakfast cereal outside the sanitarium. He had earlier developed a method for flaking corn and he now created the Battle Creek Toasted Corn Flake Company to mass-produce and market Kellogg's Toasted Corn Flakes. The cereal was an instant hit, in part because of the sanitarium's reputation, and in part because of the added malt, which made Kellogg's cereal sweeter than others.

Within a year, the Kellogg factory was producing 4,000 cases of cereal per day and still could not meet the demand. As back orders piled up, Kellogg cannily ran ads in national magazines, apologizing for the delay and asking customers to "stop buying, and give your neighbor a chance." Of course, these apology ads caused even more orders to pour into Battle Creek.

Health Food to Breakfast Food

With the company's huge success, a bitter feud erupted between the brothers over the best way to market its products. Eventually, Will gained sole rights to market the products of the Kellogg Toasted Corn Flake Co. In 1922 Will Kellogg bought out all his brother's interest in the business, changed the company's name to Kellogg Company, and scrapped some of the less-profitable products. The company grew quickly as new cereals were developed. Kellogg's All-Bran was introduced in 1915, and Rice Krispies was created in 1928.

With competition increasing in the United States, Kellogg was quick to realize the value of expanding to overseas markets. The company began selling corn flakes in Canada in 1914 and built manufacturing plants in Sydney, Australia, in 1924 and in Manchester, England, in 1938. Kellogg is also credited with creating marketing strategies like product giveaways and color magazine advertising.

Will Kellogg retired from active participation in the Kellogg Company in 1939 but remained chairman of the board until his

Kellogg Company

1876
Dr. John Wesley Kellogg takes over the Battle Creek Sanitorium.

1890
Kellogg has idea for flaked breakfast cereal.

1906
Will Kellogg founds the Battle Creek Toasted Corn Flake Company.

1914
Kellogg Company begins to sell its products to international markets.

1922
Will buys out his brother's interest in the business, changing the name to Kellogg Company.

1939
Will Kellogg retires from active participation in the company; he dies in 1951.

1996
Price war forces Kellogg to cut cereal prices by 19 percent.

2001
Kellogg has acquired Worthington Foods, Kashi Company, and Keebler.

Packaging Corn Flakes at a Kellogg's plant, circa 1950s.

death on October 6, 1951. Shortly after Will's death, Kellogg Company began producing a sweeter line of breakfast foods, including Frosted Flakes, Pop Tarts, and Fruit Loops. Kellogg's Sugar Smacks, introduced in 1953, were 56 percent sugar.

Kellogg manufactures many of the world's top-selling cereals, including Corn Flakes, Raisin Bran, Frosted Flakes, and Rice Krispies, but the competition is no less fierce now than in 1906. Years of price hikes in the 1980s and 1990s pushed cereal so high that demand fell, and politicians began to ask questions about price gouging.

In 1996 a price war erupted between Kellogg and General Mills (a subsidiary of Philip Morris), forcing Kellogg to cut cereal prices by 19 percent and reducing its market share. Challenges also emerged in the form of cheaper, store-brand knockoffs of products like Corn Flakes and Rice Krispies. However, the biggest problem Kellogg faced was the change in modern eating habits. Although cereal continues to be the most popular breakfast food, many harried consumers began to either skip breakfast or eat it on the run. Meanwhile, the public's increasing health consciousness led Kellogg to discontinue products like Rice Krispie Treats Cereal and Chocolate Chip Rice Krispies.

In early 1999 five top Kellogg executives resigned, including Kellogg's chief

Arnold Langbo, CEO of the Kellogg Company, announces price reductions on various brands of cereal during a 1996 press conference.

financial officer, its general counsel, and its head of European operations. At the same time, two groups of nuns brought attention to the company by recommending that the cereal maker stop using genetically altered crops. The company rejected the proposal but did remove genetically altered ingredients from its products in Europe and Australia, where consumer backlash over the ingredients' safety had been growing.

In April 1999 Cuban-born Carlos Gutierrez became chief executive officer of the company. He shocked Battle Creek by closing the company's hometown plant and eliminating 550 jobs in the city. He also sold the company's unsuccessful Lender's Bagels business. Gutierrez hopes to transform Kellogg from a breakfast cereal company into a healthy snack company. To this end, Kellogg began a series of acquisitions: in 1999, it acquired Worthington Foods, which makes vegetarian foods, and introduced

psyllium and oat bran products. In June 2000 the company announced that it had acquired Kashi Company, which makes products using a blend of sesame and seven whole grains. Finally, in 2001, Kellogg acquired Keebler, the second largest cookie and cracker maker in the United States, for $4.4 billion.

Further Reading

Boyle, T. Coraghessan. *The Road to Wellville*. New York: Viking, 1993.

Carson, Gerald. *Cornflake Crusade: From the Pulpit to the Breakfast Table*. New York: Arno Press and Ayer Company Publishers, 1976.

Kellogg, John Harvey. *Plain Facts for Old and Young: Embracing the Natural History and Hygiene of Organic Life*. 1879. Reprint, Buffalo, N.Y.: Heritage Press, 1974.

Money, John. *The Destroying Angel: Sex, Fitness and Food in the Legacy of Degeneracy Theory: Graham Crackers, Kellogg's Corn Flakes and American Health History*. Buffalo, N.Y.: Prometheus Books, 1998.

—Lisa Magloff

Keynes, John Maynard

1883–1946
British economist

John Maynard Keynes revolutionized economic theory during the 1930s, and his ideas formed the basis of macroeconomic policy in the West from the end of World War II until the late 1970s. No other economist has had as significant and direct an influence on the conduct of public policy.

Keynes was born in Cambridge, England, the son of Cambridge University economist and logician John Neville Keynes. He was educated at Eton, a prestigious private school, before entering Cambridge University to study mathematics. As an undergraduate he joined the Apostles, an elite club of scholars that included philosophers Bertrand Russell, G. E. Moore, and A. N. Whitehead, as well as emerging literary figures like biographer Lytton Strachey and novelist E. M. Forster. The Apostles later emerged as the core of the Bloomsbury Group of bohemian and avant-garde intellectuals, among whom Keynes remained a prominent figure.

As an undergraduate, Keynes studied with Alfred Marshall, a leading figure in the classical school of economics that Keynes would later challenge. Under Marshall's influence, Keynes drifted toward the economics profession, and in 1906 he entered the India Office of the British Civil Service. In 1909 he began teaching at King's College, Cambridge, with which he would retain an association for the rest of his life, and demonstrated potential as an economic theorist in his first book, *Indian Currency and Finance* (1913).

Keynes was a conscientious objector during World War I; he worked for the British Treasury, where he developed his critique of established economic orthodoxy in the war years. As a Treasury representative at the Versailles Peace Conference, Keynes objected to the efforts of British prime minister David Lloyd George and his French counterpart, Georges Clemenceau, to impose punitive economic damages on the defeated Germany. He resigned his position to write his polemical tract *The Economic Consequences of the Peace* (1919), in which he argued for Germany's rehabilitation and readmission into the international community, and warned that the reparations demanded by the British and the French would cause German resentment and promote a future war.

For much of the economically prosperous 1920s, Keynes worked in the private sector and made a personal fortune in the stock market. At the same time, he continued to produce innovative theories on monetary policy. When Winston Churchill, as chancellor of the Exchequer, tightened monetary policy by returning Britain to the gold standard, Keynes instantly attacked him in *The Economic Consequences of Mr. Churchill* (1925).

See also:
Great Depression; Inflation; International Monetary Fund; World Bank.

Economist John Maynard Keynes in 1925.

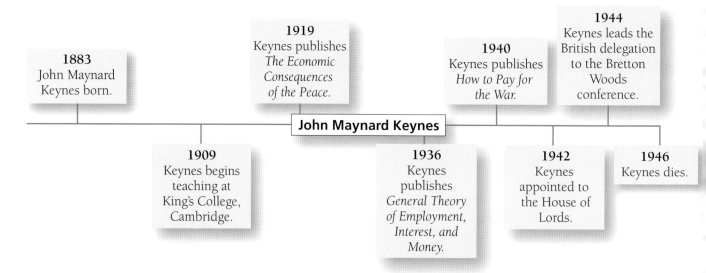

1883
John Maynard Keynes born.

1919
Keynes publishes *The Economic Consequences of the Peace.*

1940
Keynes publishes *How to Pay for the War.*

1944
Keynes leads the British delegation to the Bretton Woods conference.

John Maynard Keynes

1909
Keynes begins teaching at King's College, Cambridge.

1936
Keynes publishes *General Theory of Employment, Interest, and Money.*

1942
Keynes appointed to the House of Lords.

1946
Keynes dies.

The stock market crash of October 1929, and the subsequent Depression, seriously undermined the credibility of classical economic theory. This theory was based on Say's Law, a view advanced by the early-nineteenth-century French economist Jean-Baptiste Say, who contended that the production of goods created employment and would therefore generate sufficient economic demand for the consumption of those goods. Consequently, no long-term gluts or periods of unemployment were possible: the economy would eventually self-correct, restoring equilibrium of supply and demand.

The prolonged Depression led to a crisis of both economic theory and economic policy, as governments tried to intervene directly to tackle mass unemployment. In the United States, the Democratic administration of Franklin Delano Roosevelt, elected president in 1932, began a series of job-creation programs like the Civilian Conservation Corps and the Public Works Administration as part of an interventionist economic policy known as the New Deal.

Keynes had long protested against the view that governments should wait out economic slumps, famously writing in 1923 that "in the long run we are all dead." Keynes wrote his *General Theory of Employment, Interest, and Money* (1936) expressly to provide theoretical support for government policies designed to hasten economic recovery. He argued that during an economic downturn it was the responsibility of governments to stimulate demand. Such demand could be achieved through a reflationary combination of fiscal and monetary policies: Governments could cut taxes and thereby give consumers more money to spend, and governments could set interest rates at a suitably low level so that businesses could borrow to finance the investment necessary to meet the increased demand. Similarly, in circumstances in which inflation, rather than unemployment, was the central economic problem, governments could pursue deflationary policies by raising tax and interest rates. Consequently, Keynesian economics is frequently referred to as demand management.

Keynes's General Theory earned him a central place in British economic policy-making circles. In his pamphlet *How to Pay for*

Key Ideas of John Maynard Keynes

- Governments should actively intervene in the economy to manage the level of demand.
- Monetary policy is ineffective compared to fiscal policy in dealing with a depression.
- When demand is low, government should pursue policies to increase demand, boost employment, and raise output.
- When demand is too high, the government should pursue deflationary policies—increasing taxes and cutting spending.

he War (1940), published shortly after Britain declared war on Nazi Germany, he argued successfully for a policy of rationing and compulsory savings to avoid the price inflation threatened by the resource constraints on wartime production. He was appointed to the House of Lords in 1942, and in 1944 he led the British delegation to the Bretton Woods conference, which created the financial architecture of the postwar world, including the International Monetary Fund and the World Bank. Keynes's health had begun to fail as early as 1938, and he died in 1946.

Although Keynes himself was allied to the British Liberal Party, his ideas on macroeconomic management were widely adopted by mainstream political parties on both the right and the left of the political spectrum, and the "Keynesian Revolution" became the new economic orthodoxy of North America, Western Europe, and Scandinavia in the postwar decades. The Keynesian era witnessed unprecedented rates of economic growth but came to an end in the late 1970s, after a period of so-called "stagflation," during which both unemployment and inflation increased simultaneously. The election of Margaret Thatcher as British prime minister in 1979, and of Ronald Reagan as president of the United States in 1980, ushered in the neoliberal revolution of supply-side economics, a theory propounded by Milton Friedman and the Chicago School of Economics.

Further Reading

Felix, David. *Keynes: A Critical Life*. Westport, Conn.: Greenwood Press, 1999.

Keynes, John Maynard. *The Economic Consequences of the Peace*. 1920. Reprint, New York: Penguin Books, 1995.

———. *The General Theory of Employment, Interest, and Money*. 1935. Reprint, New York: Prometheus Books, 1997.

Moggridge, D. E. *Keynes*. 3rd ed. Toronto: University of Toronto Press, 1993.

—*Peter C. Grosvenor*

John Maynard Keynes (center) at the United Nations International Monetary Conference in 1946.

Kinko's

To anyone who has ever needed a photocopy made late at night, or to one of the estimated 20 million Americans who work from home, Kinko's is a blessing. The photocopy empire has proved that you do not have to be conventional to be successful.

Kinko's was founded in 1970 by Paul Orfalea. Dyslexic, Orfalea had a great deal of difficulty throughout school. When Orfalea attended high school in the 1960s, dyslexia was not recognized as a treatable disability, and children with dyslexia were often considered to be retarded. Orfalea's parents were supportive, and with the help of tutors he graduated from high school and attended the University of Southern California.

Orfalea majored in business but feared that his difficulty in reading would make him unemployable after college. After graduating in 1970, Orfalea moved to Isla Vista, near the University of California at Santa Barbara. "Colleges were just heaven to live near," he once explained, "so I had to figure out a way to

The first Kinko's store in Isla Vista, California, in the 1970s.

stay around one." He borrowed $5,000 from the Bank of America and rented a 100-square-foot garage behind a taco stand on Isla Vista's main thoroughfare. Orfalea called his shop Kinko's, after a nickname friends had given him in college referring to his curly red hair.

At first, Orfalea sold mostly pens and notebooks. Then, on a hunch, he leased a photocopier, a film-processing machine, and a printing press for students to use. He hired surfers and hippies to run the machines and handle any work that required reading. At night, he went door-to-door in the women's dorms, selling pens and notebooks from a backpack and trying to meet girls.

Soon the business was doing so well that Orfalea suggested to his friends that they open a Kinko's of their own. In 1972 Brad Krause, a surfer Orfalea had hired to run the printing press, opened a second Kinko's just up the California coast in San Luis Obispo, a college town well known for its surfing culture. The next year, Orfalea's cousin, Dennis Itule, opened a branch in Van Nuys, near Los Angeles. By 1975 Kinko's had 24 branches; by 1979 it had 80 branches in 28 states.

Kinko's was originally run as a decentralized confederation. Only one store was wholly owned by Kinko's Service Corporation—the parent organization for the entire chain. Instead of owning all the branches, or simply selling franchises, the parent company was involved in a cooperative relationship in which it had some stake in each store, and each store was itself a part owner of the corporation. This arrangement allowed Orfalea to maintain control over the empire while creating an incentive for plenty of local expansion.

The entire company was run in a freewheeling way. Each store catered to its particular clientele. Kinko's had 120 stores before anyone suggested giving the chain a uniform color scheme.

The flexible ownership arrangement fostered individuality, which allowed the chain to adapt quickly to changes in the marketplace. Kinko's began offering in-store computer rentals in 1986, just two years after Apple released the Macintosh, and started offering a videoconferencing service in 1994.

Lagging Behind and Catching Up

In 1985 the owner of a Kinko's store in Chicago realized that, as the staff was often working 24 hours a day to fill rush orders, the entire store might as well be open around the clock. Since then, Kinko's has attracted large numbers of loyal night owls. Kinko's also hires a large number of artists, actors, and other creative types as employees. The odd hours allow them to keep their days free for another job.

Kinko's continued to add services like color copying, faxing, and Federal Express service. It also added in-house printing and binding services and evolved from a college-oriented business into a tool for the small business and home office.

In the process, however, the Kinko's chain became unwieldy and began to lag technologically. Only in the latter half of 1994 did the company finally make 486s, Pentiums, and Power Macs widely available. Although expansion into foreign and domestic markets continued rapidly, with more

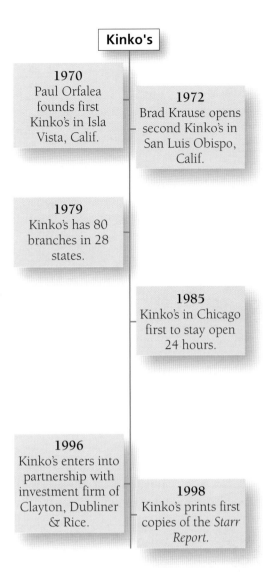

Kinko's

1970
Paul Orfalea founds first Kinko's in Isla Vista, Calif.

1972
Brad Krause opens second Kinko's in San Luis Obispo, Calif.

1979
Kinko's has 80 branches in 28 states.

1985
Kinko's in Chicago first to stay open 24 hours.

1996
Kinko's enters into partnership with investment firm of Clayton, Dubliner & Rice.

1998
Kinko's prints first copies of the *Starr Report*.

than 859 branches in the United States, Canada, Asia, and Europe by 1996, customer unhappiness was also spreading.

In 1996 Kinko's entered into a partnership with the investment firm Clayton, Dubliner & Rice, which brought in needed capital for

In second grade, I was in a Catholic school with 40 or 50 kids in my class. We were supposed to learn to read prayers and match letter blocks to the letters in the prayers. By April or May, I still didn't know the alphabet and couldn't read. I memorized the prayers so the nun thought I was reading. Finally, she figured out that I didn't even know my alphabet, and I can remember her expression of total shock that I had gotten all the way through the second grade without her knowing this. . . .

In third grade, the only word I could read was "the." I used to keep track of where the group was reading by following from one "the" to the next. . . . By seventh and eighth grade, I still had barely learned how to read. I wasn't too worried about it then because I somehow knew I'd have my own business one day, and I figured I'd hire someone to read to me.

—Paul Orfalea, *Succeeding with LD [Learning Disabilities]: Twenty True Stories about Real People with LD*

A Kinko's store at night.

upgrading the chain. In exchange for $214 million, the Wall Street firm received 41 percent of Kinko's. Orfalea kept an estimated 34 percent, and the 130 store partners in the business were allowed to swap holdings in their local operations for shares in the new company.

Clayton, Dubliner's "roll-up" plan transformed Kinko's from a decentralized confederation of locally managed stores into a smarter, sleeker, more disciplined global company. Although Orfalea still helped run the company, the management ethic had evolved from free-wheeling to establishment. A strong emphasis on employee satisfaction and training remained but was augmented by frequent mandatory training sessions and by laminated 14-step Commitments to Communication posters displayed prominently in most stores. In 1999 Kinko's was selected by *Fortune* magazine as one of the "100 Best Companies to Work for in America." The company has also begun taking publicity more seriously, instituting environmental and tree-planting programs. In 1998 Kinko's printed the first copies of the *Starr Report* on President Bill Clinton and was the first in the publishing industry to make copies available to the public. By 2000 the privately held Kinko's was worth $2 billion and had more than 25,000 employees.

Kinko's has plans for installing digital photocopiers, which use scanners and laser engines instead of light-lens technology, in all of its stores, along with digital one-hour photo labs. Kinko's started an online business, kinkos.com, in 2000, with the purchase of the existing online print business Liveprint.com. Kinko's customers are now more likely to be businesspeople who work from home than college students. Kinko's hopes to use its Web site to allow those customers to place and track orders online. Eventually, customers will be able to send documents directly from their home computers to be printed in their local store.

The company that began as a laid-back hippie enterprise now finds itself criticized for its role in driving small, mom-and-pop copy shops out of business. Kinko's is often the first chain in small towns, and some people complain that it paves the way for other chain stores. However, as long as the demand is there, Kinko's will continue to expand.

Further Reading

Imparato, Nicholas, and Oren Harari. *Jumping the Curve: Innovation and Strategic Choice in an Age of Transition.* San Francisco: Jossey-Bass Publishers, 1996.

Lauren, Jill. *Succeeding with LD [Learning Disabilities]: Twenty True Stories about Real People with LD.* Minneapolis, Minn.: Free Spirit Publishing, 1997.

—*Lisa Magloff*

Kroc, Ray

1902–1984
Founder of McDonald's franchise

Ray Kroc opened the first McDonald's franchise in 1955, and within 10 years he had hundreds of shops dotting cities and roadways in dozens of states. Kroc shaped a model for fast-food restaurants that would not only make his McDonald's franchise massively successful all over the world, but would also inspire the formation of dozens of similar restaurant chains and shopping-mall enterprises.

Kroc was born in 1902, in Oak Park, Illinois. When he was 15 years old, Kroc lied about his age and joined the Red Cross to serve as an ambulance driver in World War I. He was sent to Connecticut for training, but the war ended before he could leave for Europe. Consequently the high school dropout went to work—first as a piano player and then, in 1922, as a salesman for the Lily Tulip Cup Company.

Selling paper cups by day and playing the piano for a local radio station at night,

See also:
Assembly Line; Business Plan; Franchise; McDonald's.

Ray Kroc outside a McDonald's franchise.

Kroc emerged as a natural salesman, keen to take advantage of new opportunities. In the course of his day job he met Earl Prince, a high-volume purchaser of Lily cups, who had invented the Multimixer, a five-spindle milk shake mixer. Fascinated by the speed and efficiency of the Multimixer, Kroc entered into a deal with Prince; he mortgaged his home and invested his entire life savings to become the exclusive distributor of the Multimixer. For the next 17 years he crisscrossed the country selling the mixers.

In 1954 Kroc learned of McDonald's, a 600-square-foot restaurant in San Bernardino, California, that was using a surprising total of eight Multimixers. Always on the lookout for new business ideas, Kroc traveled to San Bernardino to find out how such a small restaurant could use so many mixers. What he found was a hamburger restaurant, but not the kind of drive-in hamburger stand that was common at the time. At McDonald's people had to get out of their cars to be served. This mode of service was part of a unique business plan implemented by Maurice and Richard McDonald, the owners of the restaurant. Their restaurant featured a limited menu, concentrating on hamburgers, cheeseburgers, french fries, soft drinks, and milk shakes. The food was of high quality, was attractively priced, and was served promptly—often within seconds—to the customers who lined up to buy it. Kroc had never seen so many people served so quickly.

When Kroc first met the McDonalds they had already established 12 McDonald's franchises in California, but Kroc envisioned a vast chain of franchises spread across America—each one equipped with eight Multimixers. He quickly proposed a deal whereby he would establish and promote new McDonald's franchises in return for a share of the franchise fees. "I was 52 years old," Kroc later observed; "I had diabetes and incipient arthritis. I had lost my gall bladder and most of my thyroid gland in earlier campaigns, but I was convinced that the best was ahead of me." Within six years he had sold 200 new franchises throughout the country.

Although the McDonald brothers had already come up with the ideas and innovations for which the chain would become famous, Kroc standardized the McDonald's operation so that it could be duplicated in every new franchise. He developed precise systems to cover every operational detail—from cooking a burger and serving a customer to washing the floors and emptying the trashcans.

Kroc also developed exact specifications for McDonald's ingredients so that the taste and cooking times would be consistent for McDonald's menu items regardless of where they were prepared. His obsession with detail was legendary. He dictated that McDonald's burgers must be exactly 3.875 inches across, weigh 1.6 ounces, and contain 19 percent fat. He even ordered all sesame seed buns to have exactly 178 seeds, and he specified how much wax there should be on the wax paper that separated one hamburger patty from another in McDonald's storage areas.

Kroc also called for standardization in matters of external design. Built to a common style and marked by the familiar golden

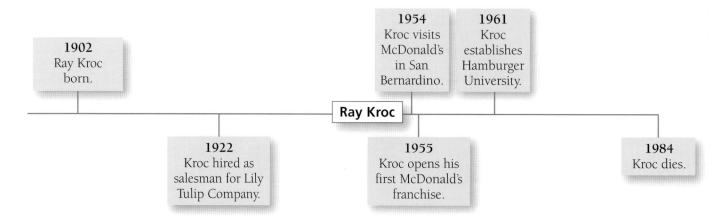

1902 Ray Kroc born.

1922 Kroc hired as salesman for Lily Tulip Company.

Ray Kroc

1954 Kroc visits McDonald's in San Bernardino.

1955 Kroc opens his first McDonald's franchise.

1961 Kroc establishes Hamburger University.

1984 Kroc dies.

arches, the McDonald's buildings themselves provided branding, suggesting to consumers that at any McDonald's they might visit they would find a common standard of quality, service, and cleanliness. Kroc was a demon for cleanliness. From the overall appearance of a franchise to its parking lot, kitchen floor, and the uniforms of its employees, he regarded cleanliness as essential. "If you have time to lean, you have time to clean," was one of his favorite maxims. To train franchise owners in this and other aspects of the McDonald's system, Kroc established Hamburger University in Oak Brook, Illinois, in 1961.

That same year Kroc bought the exclusive rights to the McDonald's concept from the McDonald brothers for $2.7 million. He was then free to run the business in his own way, but he did not make fundamental changes. He sought continued success through strict adherence to proven practices, bolstered by his own enthusiasm and his skill as a salesman.

Like other successful entrepreneurs, Kroc spotted an emerging trend in consumer demand before it became visible to others. He sensed that booming, postwar America was becoming a nation of people who would eat out with increasing frequency. He also knew that people with families needed a simple, casual restaurant with a familiar feel to it, offering friendly service, low prices, no waiting, and no reservations. In this vision he saw a place for McDonald's, and he sought to realize the vision on a grand scale. Kroc's philosophy was as blunt as a bulldozer leveling ground for the next suburban development: "It is ridiculous to call this an industry. It is not. This is rat eat rat, dog eat dog. I'll kill 'em, and I'm going to kill 'em before they kill me."

Ray Kroc's vision, enthusiasm, and capacity for action on a grand scale made McDonald's into the largest restaurant company in the world. He continued to serve McDonald's as chairman of the board from 1968 until his death in 1984.

Further Reading

Kroc, Ray, and Robert Anderson. *Grinding It Out: The Making of McDonald's*. New York: St. Martin's Paperbacks, 1987.
Love, John F. *McDonald's: Behind the Arches*. Rev. ed. New York: Bantam Books, 1995.

—*Lisa Magloff*

Ray Kroc at McDonald's offices in Chicago.

Labor Market

The labor market refers to buying and selling the services of workers. The market for labor is just as much a market as, say, the market for tomatoes or televisions. Of course, workers are not literally being bought and sold in a labor market, rather the services of the workers are being bought and sold. The labor market also differs from most other markets in other respects.

In 2002 approximately 135 million people were working in the United States, with another six million not holding a job but looking for work, adding up to a labor force equal to one-half of the U.S. population. Approximately two-thirds of all income in the United States goes to employees, with the rest going to the owners of capital (the other main factor of production) via dividends paid to shareholders, interest payments, or profits kept within a firm to be used for future projects.

This ratio has remained remarkably constant. The 140 million people who are not working or looking for work are a varied lot. They include students, retirees, homemakers, those who are institutionalized, hospitalized, or otherwise unable to work, and those who choose for whatever reason not to participate in the labor market.

Those who participate in the labor market are equally varied. In reality, markets for workers number in the millions. For instance, because of state certification requirements, those who want to buy and sell the services of a math teacher in Rutland, Vermont, have nothing to do with the market for math teachers in San Francisco, California. In addition, the market for math teachers in San Francisco is unrelated to the market for chefs in San Francisco, because buyers or sellers who participate in the market for teachers do not participate in the market for chefs.

Each market has many different buyers and sellers, each with different characteristics. For instance, the ability of computer consultants varies widely from consultant to consultant. Some who sell their services as a computer consultant can diagnose problems quickly and repair a computer in a short time, while others are better at long-term technology strategy and might struggle to find and solve problems on a specific machine or network. Likewise, some employers are very easy to work for, and offer their workers flexibility, freedom, and annual pay increases, while others seem to go out of their way to antagonize employees. Such differences do not exist in the market for televisions—Sanyo and Sony make TVs that are remarkably similar. The labor market exhibits a great amount of heterogeneity: no two workers, and no two jobs, are alike.

Economists spend a lot of time studying how firms and individuals behave in the labor market, and how government policies affect it. For instance, some economists have

See also:
Human Capital; Job Search; Occupational Safety and Health Administration.

Employment Status of U.S. Civilian Population 1960 to 2000

	Civilian labor force (in thousands)	Percent of population	Not in labor force (in thousands)	Percent of population
1960	69,628	59.4	47,617	40.6
1970	82,771	60.4	54,315	39.6
1980	106,940	63.8	60,806	36.2
1981	108,670	63.9	61,460	36.1
1982	110,204	64.0	62,067	36.0
1983	111,550	64.0	62,665	36.0
1984	113,544	64.4	62,839	35.6
1985	115,461	64.8	62,744	35.2
1986	117,834	65.3	62,752	34.7
1987	119,865	65.6	62,888	34.4
1988	121,669	65.9	62,944	34.1
1989	123,869	66.5	62,523	33.5
1990	125,840	66.5	63,324	33.5
1991	126,346	66.2	64,578	33.8
1992	128,105	66.4	64,700	33.6
1993	129,200	66.3	65,638	33.7
1994	131,056	66.6	66,758	33.4
1995	132,304	66.6	66,280	33.4
1996	133,943	63.2	66,647	33.2
1997	136,297	67.1	66,837	32.9
1998	137,673	67.1	67,547	32.9
1999	139,368	67.1	68,385	32.9
2000	140,863	67.2	68,836	32.8

Source: U.S. Bureau of the Census, *Statistical Abstract of the United States*, Bureau of the Census, Washington, D.C., 2001.

At a "pink-slip party" in Austin, Texas, in 2001, unemployed high-tech workers meet with recruiters.

come to the conclusion that making poor people pay social security taxes on their income removes their incentive to leave welfare and find work. In response, the federal government created the earned income tax credit, which gave low-income employees a subsidy to cover their taxes.

Another example of government's role in the labor market can be found in the creation of the Occupational Safety and Health Administration (OSHA). OSHA's assigned role is to regulate the working conditions in the country and improve on-the-job safety. However, some economists have argued that well-informed employees already perform this service, by requiring higher wages to do more dangerous or more difficult work. Rather than pay higher wages, many firms instead attempt to reduce the risk or unpleasantness of the work environment, achieving the very result that OSHA was designed to bring about. Economists thus debate whether an entity like OSHA is necessary.

The United States has no single labor market. When someone speaks of the labor market, he is really considering an aggregation of many smaller markets that share common characteristics and are affected by the same outside forces, but in the end function independently of one another. For example,

when the so-called dot-com boom—many Internet companies were founded in a very short period—came to an end in 2001, the technology labor market experienced a downturn, as many companies closed and others stopped hiring new workers. Were the math teacher and food-service markets mentioned above affected? Not necessarily. On the other hand, a powerful outside force like an overall downturn of the economy will affect every job market in one way or another. The labor market deserves our attention not only because nearly all of us will participate in the market at some time, but also because of its central role in the overall economy and its unique traits that distinguish it from all other markets.

Further Reading

Becker, Gary S. *Human Capital.* 3rd ed. Chicago: University of Chicago Press, 1993.

Benner, Chris. *Work in the New Economy: Flexible Labor Markets in Silicon Valley.* Malden, Mass.: Blackwell, 2002.

Card, David, and Rebecca M. Blank, eds. *Finding Jobs: Work to Welfare Reform.* New York: Russell Sage Foundation, 2000.

Hoffman, Saul D. *Labor Market Economics.* Englewood Cliffs, N.J.: Prentice-Hall, 1986.

Landsburg, Steven E. *The Armchair Economist.* New York: Free Press, 1995.

—*J. Isaac Brannon*

See also:
Collective Bargaining; Public
Sector Unionism; Strikes;
Working Conditions.

Labor Union

A labor union is an organization of workers that represents its members in negotiations with management. A union allows its members to present a single face to a company and bargain collectively, obtaining higher wages and better working conditions than would be possible if the workers bargained individually.

Beginnings of the Labor Movement
One of the earliest examples of unionlike activity can be found in the organizing of

Members of the United Auto Workers union picket a Ford Motor plant in St. Louis, Missouri, in 1937.

students at medieval universities. At the time, students paid professors for their lecture at the end of every class, and, just like today, many students were upset at the quality of the lectures. However, an individual student did not have any power over a teacher to produce a better lecture; withholding payment alone was not a sufficient penalty for a teacher to expend more effort. When an entire class banded together and threatened to withhold payments if lectures did not improve, the threat was much more potent, and the professor in such a situation would typically respond by improving his teaching.

The idea of forming a formal union has its roots in the experience of seventeenth- and eighteenth-century craftspeople. In a large city, for example, 10 or 15 different goldsmiths might be competing against one another. The goldsmiths got together and realized that if they could form some kind of cartel and reach an agreement on the prices they would charge, they could keep their prices higher and all would enjoy better incomes. Of course, any time a cartel arises, it leads to the opportunity for someone to make a great deal of money in the short run by breaking the cartel and slightly undercutting the competition. This possibility gave the craftspeople the impetus to form some sort of binding covenant among members, if not bound by law then by ideas of tradition or honor. These early craft unions, or guilds, did far more than just control prices; they established systems of apprenticeship in which skills were passed from generation to generation. They also set quality standards for materials, workmanship, and so on.

In the twentieth century, as the craftsperson gave way to the industrial worker, unions took root when workers at the same place of employment organized to petition the employer for better working conditions or higher wages. In industrial unions, workers do not organize by occupation but rather by employer. In a labor market where an employer is large enough to have some power, the firm may be able to act as

Union Members by Selected Characteristics 2000

Characteristic	Employed wage and salary workers			Median usual weekly earnings[3]			
	Total (in thousands)	Union members (percent)[1]	Represented by unions (percent)[2]	Total	Union members[1]	Represented by unions[2]	Not represented by unions
Age							
16 to 24 years old	20,166	5.0	5.7	$361	$437	$436	$355
25 to 34 years old	28,406	11.9	13.1	$550	$627	$624	$529
35 to 44 years old	32,470	14.9	16.3	$671	$716	$712	$614
45 to 54 years old	25,651	18.8	20.7	$617	$755	$752	$639
55 to 64 years old	11,204	17.8	19.6	$617	$727	$723	$592
65 years and over	2,889	8.4	9.7	$442	$577	$565	$422
Race							
White	100,455	13.0	14.4	$591	$716	$711	$565
Black	14,544	17.1	18.9	$468	$596	$590	$436
Hispanic[4]	13,609	11.4	12.8	$396	$584	$580	$377
Gender							
Men	7,884	12.3	13.5	$414	$631	$620	$394
Women	5,725	10.2	11.8	$364	$489	$492	$346
Kind of Worker							
Full-time workers	99,917	14.8	16.3	$576	$696	$691	$542
Part-time workers	20,619	6.8	7.7	NA	NA	NA	NA
Occupation							
Managerial and professional specialty	35,378	12.8	14.9	$836	$840	$834	$836
Technical sales and admin. support	36,124	8.6	9.7	$506	$598	$590	$497
Service occupations	16,953	13.2	14.4	$355	$554	$542	$327
Precision, production, craft, and repair	12,716	21.9	22.9	$613	$784	$778	$570
Operators, fabricators, and laborers	17,642	19.8	20.9	$446	$605	$602	$411
Farming, forestry, and fishing	1,974	4.5	5.5	$334	$516	$506	$325
Agricultural wage and salary workers	1,821	2.1	2.5	$347	B	B	$344
Private nonagricultural wage and salary workers	99,989	9.1	9.9	$555	$664	$657	$537
Mining	499	10.9	11.4	$768	$746	$748	$774
Construction	6,666	18.3	19.0	$584	$814	$810	$529
Manufacturing	19,167	14.8	15.6	$595	$630	$628	$587
Transportation and public utilities	7,508	24.0	25.6	$679	$768	$762	$639
Wholesale and retail trade	25,133	4.7	5.2	$444	$518	$514	$439
Finance, insurance, and real estate	7,488	1.6	2.1	$620	$596	$593	$621
Services	33,528	5.6	6.6	$543	$567	$574	$540
Government	18,976	37.5	42.0	$665	$730	$726	$609
Total	120,786	13.5	14.9	$576	$696	$691	$542

Note: Covers employed wage and salary workers 16 years old and over. B = Data not shown where base is less than 30,000. NA = Not applicable. [1] Members of a labor union or an employee association similar to a labor union. [2] Members plus workers who report no union affiliation but whose jobs are covered by a union or an employee association contract. [3] For full-time employed wage and salary workers. [4] Persons of Hispanic origin may be of any race.
Source: U.S. Bureau of Labor Statistics, *Employment and Earnings,* January 2001.

a monopsonist (a single buyer of a good or service, in this case labor) and thus pay a lower wage than would exist in a competitive labor market. In such a situation, workers and society are best served if workers form a union and prevent the firm from forcing workers to compete among themselves for the job.

While monopsonistic labor markets were not uncommon in the past (for example, the "company town," where the majority of workers in a community work for one employer), monopsonies are now exceedingly rare, at least in the United States. However, industrial unions are more practical from a bargaining perspective than craft unions, which would require an extremely high level of organization across many industries.

Unionism in the United States

The U.S. government and, indeed, a majority of the population were averse to unionization when the modern labor movement began in the late 1800s. Many viewed the modern labor movement as being hand in hand with the European socialist movement of the late nineteenth century and,

later, connected to European communists. The perceived connection with these movements made initial American attempts to form unions very difficult.

Turn-of-the-century U.S. courts vacillated on the very legality of unions. After the passage of the Sherman Antitrust Act (1890), unions were considered to be an unlawful restraint of trade for serving as a monopoly and were declared illegal for a time. Not until the Clayton Antitrust Act (1914) was passed were unions again considered legal.

The growth of unionization in the United States may not have needed the harsh economic conditions of the Depression as an impetus for growth; the workers in the manufacturing industries that formed the basis of the modern labor union had faced low wages and poor working conditions

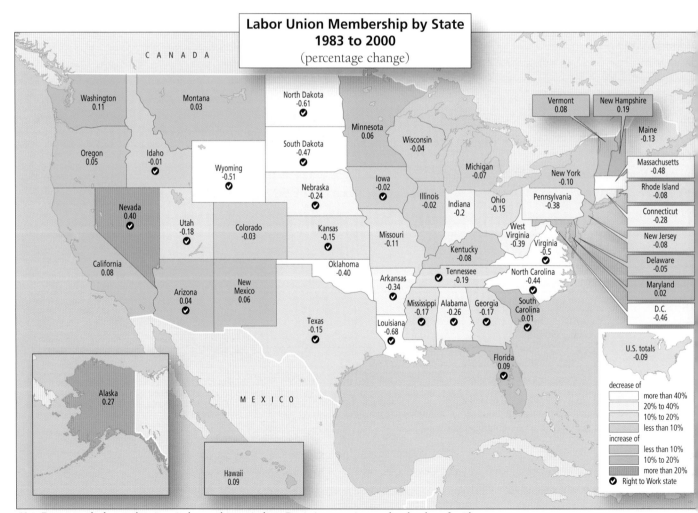

Note: For wage and salary workers in agriculture and nonagriculture. Data represent union members by place of residence.
Source: The Bureau of National Affairs, Inc., *Union Membership and Earnings Data Book: Compilations from the Current Population Survey,* Washington, D.C., 2001.

long before the terrible economic times of the 1930s. However, the Depression created a political climate more predisposed to unionism, and unions finally had a champion in the White House in Franklin D. Roosevelt, who had been elected in 1932.

Roosevelt had some help from Congress. Before he assumed office, Congress passed the Norris–LaGuardia Act (1932), which essentially took the courts out of the business of fighting unionism. In 1933 Congress passed the Davis–Bacon Act, mandating that workers receive the going union wage rate for any job done under a government contract. The original impetus for the law, which is still in force, was to prevent African Americans from taking the jobs of whites by offering to work for a lower wage. In 1935 Congress pushed through the National Labor Relations Act (also called the Wagner Act), which cemented a central role for unions in the economy by prohibiting the firing of a worker for being in a union, prohibiting firms from attempting to destroy a union, and compelling firms to bargain in good faith with a union.

Government acquiescence and a strong union leadership resulted in roughly 34 percent of the labor force in the United States being covered by a union contract by the end of the 1940s. By the 1950s that number began to fall, which it continued to do throughout the rest of the century. In 2002 only 13.5 percent of all workers belonged to a union. In the private sector, the number is below 10 percent. What precipitated the decline in unionism in the United States, when other developed nations have not experienced as protracted and steep a decline?

First, unions in the United States are concentrated in industries that have fallen in number, notably manufacturing. Over the course of the twentieth century, the relative importance of the manufacturing sector in terms of employment has fallen steadily. In 1900 18 million people were working in the service sector and roughly 8 million people were working in the manufacturing sector. Eighteen million

Is Pattern Bargaining Dead?

Pattern bargaining is the practice where union workers at plants in similar industries agree to contracts paying similar wages and benefits. For instance, when the United Auto Workers (UAW) bargains with the three leading auto companies, the real negotiations take place only with the first company that bargains with the UAW. Once the UAW reaches a contract settlement with the first company, it quickly reaches similar settlements with the other two major automakers.

For many years the UAW had practiced pattern bargaining in the construction equipment industry, which is also dominated by a handful of large companies. In the early 1990s one of those companies, Caterpillar Inc., decided that it no longer wanted to participate in pattern bargaining, believing that it could reach a better agreement by negotiating independently. Caterpillar made a final offer to the workers. When the union went on strike, the company offered its final settlement to any worker who wished to cross the picket line and brought in managers, retired white-collar workers, and hired replacement workers to run the assembly lines.

From Caterpillar's perspective the strategy worked well; productivity increased dramatically during the strike and profits grew. Finally, the UAW agreed to Caterpillar's final offer after several months and its members returned to work.

Will pattern bargaining suffer a similar death in the auto industry? While some believe that no one of the "Big Three" could find enough substitute workers for its plants, Caterpillar found no shortage of takers even in a booming economy, with workers coming from all over the country for the higher pay and the possibility of being hired full-time. Given that some assembly-line workers now make more than $100,000 a year with overtime, the wages that a strikebreaker would earn at any one of the "Big Three" would be huge. Given the sluggish performance of the auto companies, some analysts believe that a break from pattern bargaining is bound to occur in the future.

people still work in the manufacturing sector, but more than 100 million people work in the service sector.

A second reason for the decline is the success of unions in helping their workers. By obtaining higher wages and benefits, unions have in some sense contributed to the decline of jobs in the manufacturing sector. By itself, this should not be viewed as a negative; early labor leaders realized the inherent trade-off between employment and wages and were willing to sacrifice employment to improve the overall lot of workers.

Third, corporations in the United States have been more hostile to unions than in other developed countries of the West and have successfully fought the unions on many fronts. Most U.S. managers view unions as increasing costs without increasing productivity. Although unions can improve productivity (output per worker hour) by reducing turnover, handling worker grievances more

A farmer's union in Kansas in 1936.

effectively, and attracting more talented workers, unions often fight any innovation that might reduce total employment. An infamous tactic that unions employ when faced with a plant modernization is a work-to-rules strategy, where employees follow the letter of their contract in doing their assigned tasks while performing them as slowly as possible.

Fourth, unions have often lost the backing of society because of the corruption, real or perceived, of many of their leaders. For example, the Teamsters, a nationwide association of unions mainly in the trucking industry, has had several of its leaders convicted of or indicted for federal crimes and has, for a number of years, had its dealings subject to monitoring by a federal committee. The AFL-CIO, an umbrella organization encompassing nearly every union in the United States, has historically been dogged by allegations of corruption.

Finally, since World War II, unions have lost much of their government support. A series of strikes in the 1940s led Congress to pass the Taft–Hartley Act (1947), which set many limits on labor activity and also ensured that unions did not force firms to discriminate against nonunion workers. The National Labor Relations Board, which adjudicates major labor disputes, has slowly become less inclined to favor unions over time, especially during the administrations of Ronald Reagan and George H. W. Bush in the 1980s and early 1990s.

Unions and Wages

A union essentially acts as a monopoly on behalf of the employees of a firm, forcing the firm to hire all workers through the union at the negotiated wage. In essence, the union prohibits competition among workers for jobs that might lower the wage. The trade-off that any union faces when negotiating with a firm is that higher wages can mean a decrease in employment.

The extent to which wage increases will result in employment decreases is determined by the elasticity of demand for labor in a particular firm or industry. (Elasticity of labor demand refers to the responsiveness of a firm's employment to a change in wages.) In some industries, firms react to higher wages by shifting production overseas, or by mechanizing jobs formerly done by workers, or even by reducing production. Unions have been successful where firms have difficulty doing any of the above. For instance, airline pilots are some of the highest-paid union workers in the country; this is a direct result of their indispensability—airlines cannot do without them—hence a low elasticity of demand exists for pilots' services.

A criticism sometimes made of union organizing methods is that in industries where workers are poorly paid and receive scant benefits, unions are nowhere to be seen. This criticism is usually unfair; in industries like that of domestic workers, elasticity of demand is high, plus, workers can be more easily replaced. Attempts to gain higher wages for such a cohort would result in the loss of many of these jobs. In addition, the costs of organizing and running a union might not be worth the perceived benefits to workers in low-wage industries. In some instances, however, the mere threat of unionization can bring workers higher wages and benefits, as firms attempt to

Teamster leader Jimmy Hoffa addresses 10,000 union members at New York City's Madison Square Garden in 1960.

In 1997 thousands of culinary workers rally in front of the New York, New York, Hotel and Casino in Las Vegas, in support of the resort's restaurant workers, who were trying to unionize.

address any dissatisfaction that might lead to union organizing.

The irony of unions is that the more successful they are in procuring high wages, better benefits, and safer working conditions, the more jobs they eventually lose, as firms ultimately find mechanization more profitable. For instance, automobile plants are now highly automated and make only a small proportion of their own parts; this transformation is partly a result of the high wages and benefits that the United Auto Workers has been able to obtain for its members.

Further Reading

Freeman, Richard, and James Medoff. *What Do Unions Do?* New York: Basic Books, 1984.

Green, Max. *Epitaph for American Labor: How Union Leaders Lost Touch with America.* Washington, D.C.: AEI Press, 1996.

Mauer, Michael. *The Union Member's Complete Guide: Everything You Want—and Need—to Know about Working Union.* Annapolis, Md.: Union Communications Services, 2001.

Nelson, Daniel. *Shifting Fortunes: The Rise and Decline of American Labor, from the 1820s to the Present.* Chicago: Ivan R. Dee, 1998.

—J. Isaac Brannor

Landrum–Griffin Act

In 1959 the U.S. Congress passed the Labor–Management Reporting and Disclosure Act, more commonly known as the Landrum–Griffin Act. The law, an attempt to make unions more responsive to the needs of their members, resulted from a congressional investigation into the practices of several union officials. This landmark legislation gave the federal government the right to oversee the internal administration of labor unions, created a worker's "Bill of Rights" to promote democratic procedures and reduce union corruption, and placed severe restrictions on the ability of unions to conduct secondary boycotts and organizational picketing. Critics of the act believe it radically skewed the odds in favor of management and against labor.

The Landrum–Griffin Act is one of three key laws that shaped federal policies involving organized labor during the twentieth century. The first, the National Labor Relations Act (Wagner Act), was passed in 1935. Among its provisions, the Wagner Act outlawed several practices management used to discourage union activity. Following passage of the Wagner Act, union membership soared from approximately nine million in 1935 to nearly 17 million by the mid-1950s.

The second major labor law was passed after World War II when thousands of workers went on strike seeking wage and benefit increases denied them during the war. In this postwar era, anticommunist sentiment ran very high, and public opinion began to turn against organized labor, which was perceived by some as having socialist or communist connections. The result was passage of the Labor–Management Relations Act (Taft–Hartley Act) in 1947, which limited union power by banning the closed (union-only) shop and allowing states to enact right-to-work laws.

Although the Taft–Hartley Act was a major setback for unions, organized labor continued to grow in strength, and by 1953 nearly one-third of all workers in the United States were union members. As organized labor grew in size, some union officials, including Jimmy Hoffa of the International Brotherhood of Teamsters, abused their power and engaged in financial mismanagement for personal gain. As allegations of union corruption grew, the Senate formed the McClellan Committee in 1957 to investigate. Its hearings, which lasted 270 days, uncovered evidence of collusion between dishonest employers and union officials, the use of violence by certain segments of labor leadership, and the diversion and misuse of labor union funds by high-ranking officials. The hearings also produced sharp and colorful exchanges between witnesses like Hoffa and Chairman McClellan or the committee's chief counsel, Robert F. Kennedy.

See also:
Collective Bargaining; Labor Union; National Labor Relations Act; Strikes; Taft–Hartley Act; Teamsters Union.

Landrum–Griffin Act: Worker Bill of Rights	
Equal rights	
Gives every member of a labor organization the right to:	
Nominate candidates	
Vote in elections or referendums	
Attend meetings	
Participate in the deliberations of meetings	
Freedom of speech and assembly	
Protects member's right to:	
Meet freely with other members	
Express opinions on candidates or organization business	
Dues, initiation fees, and assessments	
Stipulates that dues and initiation fees cannot be increased except:	
In the case of a local labor organization	
By majority vote by secret ballot after reasonable notice	
In the case of a national organization	
By majority vote of the delegates at a convention held on not less than 30 days' written notice	
By majority vote of members voting in secret ballot	
By majority of members of the governing board as provided by the organization's constitution, such action to be effective only until the next regular convention of the organization	
Protection of the right to sue	
Prohibits labor organizations from restricting members' right to sue	
Safeguards against improper disciplinary action	
Forbids disciplinary action unless the member has been:	
Served with written specific charges	
Given a reasonable time to prepare his defense	
Afforded a full and fair hearing	

Landrum–Griffin Act
(Excerpt)

(1) **Equal rights**

Every member of a labor organization shall have equal rights and privileges within such organization to nominate candidates, to vote in elections or referendums of the labor organization, to attend membership meetings, and to participate in the deliberations and voting upon the business of such meetings, subject to reasonable rules and regulations in such organization's constitution and bylaws.

(2) **Freedom of speech and assembly**

Every member of any labor organization shall have the right to meet and assemble freely with other members; and to express any views, arguments, or opinions; and to express at meetings of the labor organization his views, upon candidates in an election of the labor organization or upon any business properly before the meeting, subject to the organization's established and reasonable rules pertaining to the conduct of meetings: Provided, that nothing herein shall be construed to impair the right of a labor organization to adopt and enforce reasonable rules as to the responsibility of every member toward the organization as an institution and to his refraining from conduct that would interfere with its performance of its legal or contractual obligations.

The public outcry for reform resulting from the McClellan Committee hearings provided the impetus for passing the Landrum–Griffin Act. The most significant and controversial sections of the law are Title I, which created a worker's "Bill of Rights," and Title VII, which tightened restrictions on union interactions with employers. Because the McClellan Committee uncovered instances of unions denying their members basic rights, the Landrum–Griffin Act requires every labor organization to adopt a constitution that guarantees its members freedom of speech and assembly, the right to vote in periodic secret elections, as well as the right to review union dues. Furthermore, members have the right to sue the union if they feel these rights are violated.

Title VII amended the Taft–Hartley Act by significantly restricting the use by unions of boycott and picketing. Specifically, conducting secondary boycotts (an organized refusal to purchase the products of, or do business with, a company that is doing business with another company where the employees are in a labor dispute) was made more difficult for unions. The law also placed bans on several forms of picketing, including coercive picketing and extortionate picketing, as well as severe restrictions on organizational picketing, which was used to force employers to recognize a union. Other sections of the law established minimum reporting and financial disclosure requirements for all unions, restricted the ability of a union to interfere in the affairs of its locals, and set standards for all elected union officials.

Landrum–Griffin continued the legislative trend, begun under Taft–Hartley, of restricting union picketing and boycotts. In the wake of Landrum–Griffin, strike activity declined, union membership began to drop, and the labor movement overall became more cooperative with management. Staunch critics of the act argue that it undermined the labor movement in the guise of democratizing it.

Further Reading

Bellace, Janice R., and Alan D. Berkowitz. *The Landrum–Griffin Act: Twenty Years of Federal Protection of Union Members' Rights*. Philadelphia University of Pennsylvania Press, 1979.

Bloom, Gordon F., and Herbert R. Northrup. *Economics of Labor Relations*. 9th ed. Homewood, Ill.: Richard D. Irwin, 1981.

Lee, R. Alton. *Eisenhower & Landrum–Griffin: A Study in Labor-Management Politics*. Lexington: University Press of Kentucky, 1990.

—David Mason

Lands' End

Lands' End is known primarily as a direct (mail order) merchant. With revenues topping $1.3 billion in 2000, Lands' End ranked fifteenth in sales among its competitors, but many customers rank it first in innovation and high standards, an enviable reputation in a frequently maligned industry. Known for principled business practices and inventive adaptations to emerging technology and markets, the company credits its success to old-fashioned ingredients: good employees and good merchandise.

The company was founded in the early 1960s by Gary Comer. As he tells the story, the idea came to him when he was 33 years old, traveling in the Swiss Alps and wondering what he should do with his life. He should, he decided, start a business centered on his hobby, sailboat racing. Having won or placed in three world sailboat racing competitions, Comer was no novice, and he believed he could somehow profit from the expertise he had developed.

Comer returned to the United States and entered into a business relationship with an established sail maker, Dick Stearns.

He and Stearns began selling sails out of a creaky loft on Chicago's northwest side. When Comer saw that his customers often needed sailboat fittings as well as sails, he brought new partners into the business and expanded his line of products. In deciding what to name his new company, Comer recalls, he sat down one day with a pencil and paper to brainstorm a list of ideas. From this list he settled on Lands' End; he thought it conjured romantic visions of the sea and distant places. Over the years, people have asked Comer why the apostrophe in the company name is improperly placed. Comer concedes he simply made a mistake—but one he has grown to like; he believes the evidence of human error also gives the company a personal, human quality. In the spring of 1963 five partners incorporated Lands' End Yacht Stores, Inc.

Early on, the partners sold their merchandise through magazine ads, but by their second year of operations they had created their first catalog, Lands' End Yachtsman's Equipment Guide. Employing only a handful of people, the fledgling company processed 15 orders on a good day. Yet, from the beginning, these owners and employees took their work seriously,

See also:
Business Plan; Customer Service; Retail and Wholesale.

Lands' End founder Gary Comer in an undated photo.

intending to provide first-rate customer service and the highest-quality merchandise at the best price.

Through the 1960s and into the 1970s, the company grew and its merchandise line expanded, but these were decades in which mail order businesses were not highly esteemed by the public. A former Lands' End executive recalls his effort to soften that negative perception by replacing the old term *mail order* with a new term: *direct merchants*. The new term, he said, likened the company's business practices to those of the ancient sea merchants and presented a conceptually pleasing, old-fashioned image of world-class goods and face-to-face, one-on-one customer dealings.

The Lands' End owners eventually outgrew their space in Chicago and moved the plant to Dodgeville, a small town in rural Wisconsin, in 1978. It seemed to be a striking setting initially because of its pastoral beauty, but it soon served Lands' End well for reasons other than the aesthetic. Lands' End found that people in the Dodgeville area made excellent employees. As farmers and children of farmers, they were early risers, accustomed to working hard, and they took pride in doing their work well. Comer praised his workers for their high standards, observing that whether their work involved trimming canvas for luggage or hemming pants to customers' specifications, their performance was always first-rate.

Specific business principles have informed the company's practice throughout its more than 30 years of successful operations. The first principle is to find high-quality merchandise. Under the Lands' End business plan, a new supplier of goods is asked how a product can be made better, never how it can be made cheaper. Merchandise is always purchased directly from the manufacturer or made on the Lands' End premises—no middlemen, no high-priced brand-name labels. Next the merchandise is honestly priced; the company does not believe in an initial, artificial markup so that a phony sale can be held in the future. To handle and sell the merchandise, the company hires only hard-working, smart, friendly employees; then it pays them well and rewards them with a share in the company's profits. When orders are received, merchandise is shipped immediately, generally on the following day. Finally, all merchandise arrives with a full no-questions-asked guarantee that is good for all time and under all circumstances.

In addition to its principled practices, the company is distinguished by attention to innovation and service. Lands' End was the first company to offer a toll-free number to its catalog customers. Today those phone lines are open 24 hours a day, 364 days a year. In addition to operators who take orders, the company offers "Specialty Shoppers"—personable staff members who are available 16 hours per day to help customers select the right size, find the right gift, or choose the right accessories. The company entered the Internet sales market in 1995. In an effort to offer more, not less

Lands' End

1963
Lands' End incorporated.

1964
Lands' End issues first catalog.

1978
Lands' End moves plant to Dodgeville, Wisconsin.

1978
Lands' End becomes first company to establish a toll-free catalog number.

1995
Lands' End launches Web site.

2002
Lands' End purchased by Sears for $1.9 billion.

Shipping packages at the Lands' End warehouse.

customer contact and customer satisfaction, a Web site was designed to feature Lands' End Live, an interactive customer chat service, and My Virtual Model™, which allows customers to "try on" clothing electronically, using an animated model that approximates different body types.

In 2002 Sears purchased Lands' End for $1.9 billion. The $62-a-share purchase price was considered by most analysts to be a very good value for Lands' End shareholders. The acquisition permitted the Dodgeville operation to expand and allowed brand marketing to move beyond the somewhat saturated mail-order market into Sears' 870 retail department stores. Sears was attracted by the sophisticated and successful e-commerce model of Lands' End and the decidedly upscale appeal of its clothing.

Further Reading

"Lands' End Improves Online Profitability via My Virtual Model Technology." *Direct Marketing*, June 2001.

"Lands' End Tacks Again." *Business Week*, 14 December 1998, 90–98.

Tedeschi, Bob. "Selling Made-to-Order Clothing Online without Sending the Customer to a Tailor. " *New York Times*, 5 November 2001.

—*Karen Ehrle*

Lansing, Sherry

1944–
Film executive

Widely considered to be one of the most powerful women in Hollywood, Sherry Lansing has been the chairwoman of Paramount Pictures, the movie division of media conglomerate Viacom, for almost a decade. A veteran of the movie business, Lansing became the first woman to head a major studio in 1980 when she was appointed president of production at 20th Century-Fox.

Paramount Pictures CEO Sherry Lansing.

High-ranking female executives are no longer an anomaly in Hollywood. As Lansing built her career, however, her gender and demeanor made her both a curiosity and a controversial figure. Despite criticism from all sides, Lansing's perseverance and talent for picking popular movies has assured her a secure place at the top of an industry known for rapid turnover.

Lansing was born in Chicago, Illinois, on July 31, 1944, to David and Margo Duehl. Lansing's mother was a German Jew who fled the Holocaust; her father was a fan of the performing arts, including the movies, who owned a number of apartment buildings. When Lansing was nine years old, her father died. Her mother married a businessman named Norton Lansing three years later, and she and her two daughters took Lansing's name.

Lansing attended Northwestern University, where she graduated with a theater degree in 1966. By then she had married her high school sweetheart, the future plastic surgeon Michael Brownstein. Lansing and Brownstein moved to Los Angeles so Brownstein could complete a medical internship and Lansing could pursue her dream of becoming a movie actress.

Once in Los Angeles, Lansing taught English and math part-time in East Los Angeles. She quit teaching after she was assaulted by a student while she tried to break up a fight. She had more success with acting. A tall, statuesque brunette with striking blue eyes, Lansing had been modeling since high school. In Los Angeles she found work in television commercials for beauty products and landed guest spots on a variety of television shows. In 1970 she received roles in the movies *Rio Lobo* and *Loving*. Despite these successes, Lansing found that she did not enjoy acting; this realization, together with the failure of her marriage to Brownstein, left her looking for a new direction. She began dating producer Ray Wagner, who discovered her talent for recognizing a good script and fixing the flaws in a bad one. He hired her as a script reader, and eventually she began reading scripts for other producers as well. In 1975 she went to work for

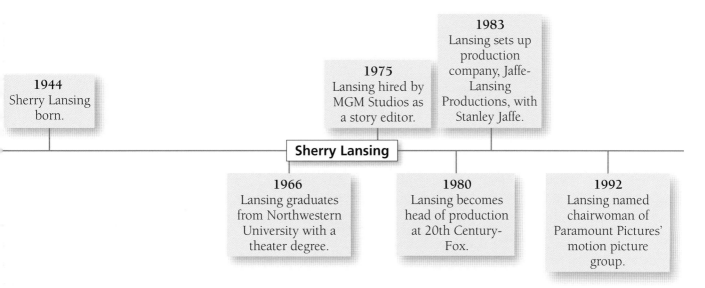

1944
Sherry Lansing born.

1966
Lansing graduates from Northwestern University with a theater degree.

1975
Lansing hired by MGM Studios as a story editor.

1980
Lansing becomes head of production at 20th Century-Fox.

1983
Lansing sets up production company, Jaffe-Lansing Productions, with Stanley Jaffe.

1992
Lansing named chairwoman of Paramount Pictures' motion picture group.

Sherry Lansing

MGM Studios as an executive story editor, hired by another producer and former boyfriend, Dan Melnick. Two years later, she was hired as senior vice president of production at Columbia Pictures. Although Lansing oversaw successful movies including *Kramer vs. Kramer,* she also hit what is known as the glass ceiling: she was told by the studio's president that she would never be promoted to head of production because men would not work for a woman. Melnick persuaded 20th Century-Fox to be less rigid, however, and in 1980, at age 35, Lansing was hired as head of production.

Lansing's move to 20th Century-Fox was well covered in the media because she was the first woman to hold such a high position in the male-dominated world of Hollywood. Lansing's graciousness and charm were duly noted—it is often joked that she is the only person in Hollywood with no enemies—but her appointment was controversial nonetheless. Unlike some female executives of the period who acted in a stereotypically masculine way, Lansing had a girlish, even flirtatious way of acting in addition to good looks. Although she tried to downplay her sexuality by wearing drab outfits, the fact that her big career move had been facilitated by a man she had once dated (albeit long after she stopped dating him) gave rise to rumors. The irony of the publicity surrounding Lansing's rise is that she was reportedly not especially excited about the 20th Century-Fox job. She had been considering a different move,

into producing, when the offer from 20th Century-Fox arrived, and she felt that she should accept in order to open a door for other female executives.

Once she began working at 20th Century-Fox, Lansing discovered that, despite her title, she had little actual power. The situation worsened in 1981, when Denver oilman Marvin Davis bought the studio. Although the buyout made Lansing wealthy, Davis was so unused to the idea of female executives that when he first met Lansing he assumed she was the studio president's secretary. In this context Lansing found that her judgments about movies were frequently overruled. For example, 20th Century-Fox produced the hit film *Chariots of Fire* but, over Lansing's objections, the studio did not distribute the film because her superiors thought it would flop. Instead, the film won the Academy Award for best picture in 1981.

By 1983 Lansing had had enough. She resigned from 20th Century-Fox and set up a production company with former Columbia Pictures president Stanley Jaffe. Jaffe-Lansing Productions made some of the most talked-about movies of the 1980s, including *Fatal Attraction,* about a woman who stalks a married man with whom she had an affair, and *The Accused*, about a woman who was gang-raped. Lansing demonstrated that she had a knack for producing commercially successful films that also sparked debates about serious issues.

Mel Gibson stars in Braveheart *(1995).*

Jaffe left the production company in 1991 to accept an appointment as president and chief operating officer of Paramount Pictures. A year later, Lansing joined him at Paramount as chairwoman of the motion picture group, replacing Brandon Tartikoff, a former television executive who had overseen Paramount's television and movie businesses. Lansing had refused Jaffe's earlier requests to join Paramount, but in 1991 she married her second husband, director William Friedkin, and she wanted a job where she did not have to go on location wherever a movie was being shot.

At Paramount, Lansing discovered that the studio had almost no movies in the pipeline. In a flurry of activity, she put out several movies on an accelerated schedule, including *Forrest Gump, Braveheart, Saving Private Ryan* (coproduced with Dream Works), and *Titanic* (coproduced with 20th Century-Fox). These critical and commercial successes boosted Paramount's market share and helped to restore it as a force in the film industry.

Further Reading

Abramowitz, Rachel. *Is That a Gun in Your Pocket? Women's Experience of Power in Hollywood.* New York: Random House, 2000.

Hall, Carla. "The 'Ties' That Don't Bind: Sherry Lansing on Her New Film and Her Passion for Producing." *The Washington Post*, 20 September 1992, G1.

Welkos, Robert. "Every Day Was High Noon." *Los Angeles Times*, 22 August 1993, Calendar section, p. 8.

—*Mary Sissor*

Lauder, Estée

1908–
Founder, Estée Lauder, Inc.

Estée Lauder was one of the significant entrepreneurs in the cosmetics industry. Lauder started her business by making skin creams in her kitchen and built her corporation through innovative, widely imitated marketing strategies and by developing new product lines to satisfy changing consumer tastes. By 2000 Estée Lauder, Inc., was an international corporation with annual sales of several billion dollars and Lauder's personal fortune was estimated at more than $5 billion.

Estée Lauder was born Josephine Esther Mentzer in 1908 in the borough of Queens in New York City, the youngest child of Hungarian immigrant parents. As a child, she worked in her father's hardware store and in a small department store owned by relatives. These experiences probably stimulated her desire to establish her own business but, according to her autobiography, the greatest influence on her career was her uncle John Schotz. In 1924 Schotz started a small business manufacturing skin creams and other chemical preparations. Esty, as she was called, spent all her free time with her uncle and soon began experimenting with her own formulas. Uncle John also taught her to give facial massages and to make up women's faces. She practiced on her high school classmates and used her skills to demonstrate her uncle's cosmetics in neighborhood beauty parlors.

Esty married Joe Lauter in 1930 and in 1933 gave birth to a son, Leonard. In addition to being a wife and mother, she operated a home-based business, making beauty creams and selling them primarily in beauty parlors. She offered customers free makeovers, applying cleansing oil and creams, followed by powder, rouge, and lip color. She also distributed free samples of her products. Both beauty makeovers and free samples remained important parts of the Lauder marketing strategy and have become standard thoughout the industry.

By 1937 Esty Lauter had changed her name to Estée Lauder and had begun selling her cosmetics under that name. She made contacts among the wealthy women of New York City and marketed her products at Manhattan bridge parties and at

See also:
Women in the Workforce.

Estée Lauder in New York in 1962.

expensive hotels. Believing in the importance of an upper-class image for her cosmetics, she learned to dress and speak as her wealthy clients did and concealed the fact that she had been born to a relatively poor family. In 1939 she divorced her husband and moved to Miami Beach, Florida, where she opened a shop in an expensive hotel. However, in 1942 she remarried Joe Lauter and gave birth to a second son, Ronald. In 1946 Lauder and her husband founded Estée Lauder Cosmetics. They divided company responsibilities, Estée marketing the products while Joe handled manufacturing and finances.

To promote an upscale image the company distributed cosmetics through high-end department stores rather than drugstores and supermarkets. This marketing strategy also fit the company's small budget, which did not allow for a national advertising campaign. The company's first major department store relationship was with Saks Fifth Avenue in New York City. Lauder convinced the department store's reluctant cosmetics buyer to stock Lauder products by donating Estée Lauder lipsticks as table gifts at a charity luncheon where the buyer was speaking. At the conclusion of the luncheon, many of the women who had received the free lipsticks crossed the street to Saks in search of other Lauder products, and Saks quickly placed an order. Within a few years, Estée Lauder cosmetics were sold in exclusive department stores all over the country.

Lauder planned each new department store account meticulously. She observed that most customers looked to the right as they entered a store, and insisted on a location in that area. She trained saleswomen to do free customer makeovers. Invitations to visit the counter and receive free samples were sent. Customers were also promised a free gift when they made a purchase. Competitors at first predicted that the Lauders' company would go broke, but other cosmetics firms soon began to imitate these strategies.

The company's first great success came in 1953 with the introduction of Youth Dew, a scented liquid that could be used either as a perfume or a bath oil. Lauder was aware that few women at that time purchased perfume for themselves; they usually received it as a gift and wore it only on special occasions. Because Youth Dew was a bath oil, and because it was sold at a lower price than most prestige perfumes, women did not consider it a luxury. They bought it themselves and used it daily. Youth Dew turned Estée Lauder Cosmetics into a multimillion-dollar industry.

Over the following years, several new fragrances were introduced under the Estée Lauder brand, most created at a new research and development laboratory. Each introduction included department store promotional events, training of sales people, and national advertising. Expenses were high, and most of the company's profits were reinvested in the

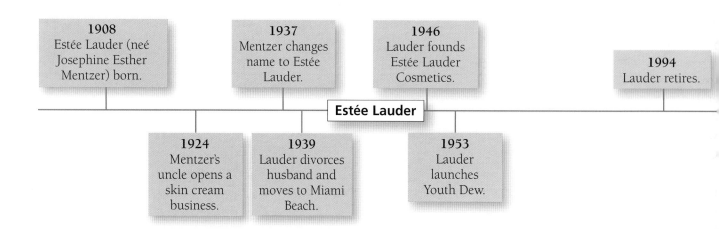

1908
Estée Lauder (neé Josephine Esther Mentzer) born.

1937
Mentzer changes name to Estée Lauder.

1946
Lauder founds Estée Lauder Cosmetics.

1994
Lauder retires.

Estée Lauder

1924
Mentzer's uncle opens a skin cream business.

1939
Lauder divorces husband and moves to Miami Beach.

1953
Lauder launches Youth Dew.

business, but the result was a constantly growing company.

In 1960 Lauder began to set up cosmetics counters in prestigious European department stores like Harrods in London and the Galeries Lafayette in Paris. By the year 2000 Estée Lauder's international division sold products in more than 100 countries. The Lauder company also began to add new brands of products, including Aramis, a line of men's toiletries; Clinique, which emphasizes healthy skin care; and Origins, based on natural ingredients.

Estée Lauder retired from the company in 1994. Her success was based on hard work, creative ideas, and great enthusiasm for the beauty industry, combined with close and continuous study of the changing desires of consumers.

Further Reading

Gavenas, Mary Lisa. *Color Stories: Behind the Scenes of America's Billion-Dollar Beauty Industry.* New York: Simon & Schuster, 2002.

Gobé, Marc. *Emotional Branding: The New Paradigm for Connecting Brands to People.* New York: Allworth Press, 2001.

Israel, Lee. *Estée Lauder—Beyond the Magic.* New York: Macmillan Publishing, 1985.

Koehn, Nancy F. "Estée Lauder," in *Brand New: How Entrepreneurs Earned Consumers' Trust from Wedgwood to Dell.* Boston: Harvard Business School Press, 2001.

Lauder, Estée. *Estée—A Success Story.* New York: Random House, 1985.

—*Jean Caldwell*

A Clinique saleswoman tests makeup on a customer at a counter in the Asahikawa Seibu department store in Hokkaido, Japan.

See also:
Business Cycles; Inflation;
Unemployment.

Leading Economic Index

The Leading Economic Index (LEI) is the most widely watched and reported of the economic indicators. Other economic indicators include the Coincident Index and Lagging Index. Each index is a composite, made up of a number of economic statistics called indicators. The Coincident (happening at the same time) and Lagging (happening after) Indexes confirm the location of the business cycle, but the LEI shows where the business cycle is going.

A nonprofit business research firm, the Conference Board, compiles the economic indicators every month. The Conference Board has been gathering this data since December 1995. From 1965 to 1995, the U.S. Department of Commerce gathered the information. The Conference Board was founded in 1916 to provide economic and business research. In addition to the Economic Indicator series, it also reports the Consumer Confidence Index and a number of other domestic and global data series.

Investors use the information in the LEI to anticipate changes in stock and bond prices. Policy makers, including the Federal Reserve, use the information when making decisions about raising or lowering interest rates or changing the money supply. Businesses can use the information to anticipate changing demand and adjust their inventories. Careful interpretation of the LEI is necessary. One must consider the size of the movement, for how many months it has been increasing or decreasing, and how many and which of the composite indicators have changed.

Unlike many other measures, an index is unitless; it is measured in points, not dollars or tons or inches, and thus it has meaning only when compared with itself. Each measure sets a base year when the index equals 100. The LEI's base year is 1992. Monthly reports of an index indicate whether it has moved up or down, by how much in absolute and percentage terms, and how the current month's index number compares with historical values.

All of the economic indicators are composite indexes—they are an average of the separate economic statistics in each category. Any one of the composite statistics may be volatile; by grouping the statistics together in one index and averaging the measures, a smoother series is produced.

The LEI

The LEI is a composite index made up of 10 data series that are believed to move up before the business cycle does. The components of the LEI are: average weekly hours in manufacturing, average weekly initial claims for unemployment benefits, manufacturers' new orders for consumer goods and materials, vendor performance,

Components of the Leading Economic Index

Employment	Production	Business Activity
Average weekly hours in manufacturing	Manufacturers' new orders for consumer goods and materials	Vendor performance
Average weekly initial claims for unemployment benefits	Manufacturers' new orders for nondefense capital goods	Standard & Poor's 500
	New private housing building permits	Money supply
	Index of Consumer Expectations	10-year Treasury bond interest rate spread

manufacturers' new orders for nondefense capital goods, new private housing building permits, stock prices for 500 common stocks, money supply, 10-year Treasury bond interest rate spread, and the Index of Consumer Expectations.

The elements of the LEI fall into three groups: employment, production, and business activity. Employment is measured by average workweek and unemployment claims. If business is picking up, then hours worked will increase and layoffs as measured by unemployment claims will go down. Businesses will expand hours and call back workers before hiring new employees. (New hires are part of the Coincident Index.)

Production measures look at what may be coming in the manufacturing and construction sectors. Orders for consumer goods signal increasing consumer demand. Manufacturers order new capital equipment, like machines, before they increase production. An increase in building permits indicates new housing and eventually new appliances and furniture to go in the new housing. The Index of Consumer Expectations, calculated by the University of Michigan's Survey Research Center, provides another indication of consumers' purchase plans for the near future. All of these indicators will change before actual production does, rising before production increases, thus making them leading indicators. (Actual production and sales figures are part of the Coincident Index.)

The third category of the LEI looks at business activity. Vendor performance, or wait time, for deliveries to factories will increase as the number of orders increases. Stock prices of the Standard & Poor's 500 will also rise as economic activity increases. Money supply, also called broad money, includes cash and money available in checking and saving accounts. An increase in money supply happens when banks increase lending. More money lent means borrowers are spending, investing, or starting their own business ventures. All are good indicators of economic growth.

Components of the Coincident Index
Coincident Index
• Employees on nonagricultural payrolls
• Personal income less transfer payments
• Industrial production
• Manufacturing and trade sales

The Coincident and the Lagging Indexes

The Coincident Index moves with the business cycle, increasing or decreasing at the same rate as gross domestic product (GDP). The four coincident indicators are: number of employees on nonagricultural payrolls, industrial production, personal income minus transfer payments, and manufacturing and trade sales volume. Because GDP measures the sales of new final goods and services, it will increase as industrial production and sales increase. The same is true with employment and income figures; they increase as output increases and more workers are needed to make additional goods. Only wages and salaries (income) are included; government payments (transfer payments) are not counted. Examples of transfer payments are unemployment benefits and social security checks.

The third and final component of the Economic Indicators is the Lagging Index. Lagging indicators change after the business cycle has turned, falling after GDP has begun to decline and rising after GDP has begun to increase. Seven economic statistics make up the Lagging Index: average duration of

Components of the Lagging Index
Lagging Index
• Average duration of unemployment
• Inventory to sales ratio
• Labor cost per unit of output
• Average prime lending rate
• Amount of commercial and industrial loans
• Ratio of consumer credit debt to personal income
• Inflation as measured by the consumer price index

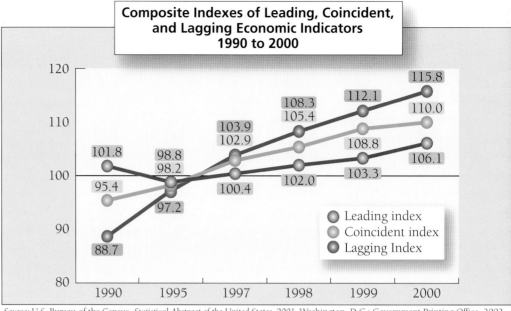

Composite Indexes of Leading, Coincident, and Lagging Economic Indicators 1990 to 2000

- Leading index
- Coincident index
- Lagging Index

Source: U.S. Bureau of the Census, *Statistical Abstract of the United States, 2001,* Washington, D.C.: Government Printing Office, 2002.

unemployment, inventory to sales ratio, labor cost per unit of output, average prime lending rate, amount of commercial and industrial loans, ratio of consumer credit debt to personal income, and inflation as measured by the consumer price index. The lagging indicator index tells economic policy makers the strength or weakness of an economic expansion or contraction.

Inflation tends to increase after an expansion has begun, especially as the labor cost per unit of output goes up. As firms try to hire more workers to increase production, they eventually run low on people to hire. Businesses then increase wages to try to get more workers. This increases the labor costs for each unit made by a firm. As labor costs go up, firms need to increase the price of goods to maintain profits. Increasing wages and prices leads to inflation. The number of loans and interest rates will also rise after an expansion is under way. Businesses become more certain the economy is really picking up and borrow money to expand factories or start new product lines. As more and more businesses begin expanding, demand for loans will increase, pushing up the cost of loans, or the interest rate. The reverse is true, when the economy contracts into a recession.

The economic indicators require careful interpretation. Signs of an upturn in GDP from the LEI give businesses and investors time to buy or sell stocks and increase inventories. Because the timing is imprecise, however, investors do not know if the change will occur in three months, nine months, or even at all. The indicators are only as good as their components. Any problems or biases in the individual statistics will influence the composite index. Using many overlapping economic indicators, including production and sales figures, helps reduce error. The indicators have been changed over time, dropping some components and adding others to try to get the best possible index. Reporting of indicators can also create a self-fulfilling prophecy. If the LEI indicates a recession is coming, businesses may slow down, cutting back production and hours. Reduced hours cuts workers' income. Workers will then reduce spending, creating the slowdown predicted.

Further Reading

Bronfenbrenner, Martin. *Economics.* 2nd ed. Boston: Houghton Mifflin, 1987.

Conference Board. http://www.globalindicators.org (February 13, 2003).

Frumkin, Norman. *Guide to Economic Indicators.* 3rd ed. Armonk, N.Y.: M.E. Sharpe, 2000.

Sowell, Thomas. *Basic Economics: A Citizen's Guide to the Economy.* New York: Basic Books, 2001.

—Donna Miller

Legal Services

Lawyers are given the power to defend and protect persons within the set of rules and regulations that are the law of the land. Lawyers can also argue how laws might be interpreted, elaborated, or altered to benefit their clients. Abraham Lincoln, who practiced law before being elected president, noted that because all people seek the best possible lives, the land is well populated with lawyers.

In Lincoln's day the legal profession was a humble one. A typical law office in the 1800s had a practitioner with perhaps one associate or partner. Young people wanting to become lawyers apprenticed themselves to established lawyers. The first law school in the United States had been established in 1774 and the first university law school opened at Harvard in 1817, but in general law schools were not popular places to learn the trade. During the Civil War fewer than 1,000 students were enrolled in law schools, with most studying at small schools of dubious quality that offered courses of two years or less. In the 1890s less than 20 percent of lawyers were thought to have attended law school.

At the end of the nineteenth century, changing social conditions led to a change in the way lawyers were trained. Massive immigration to the United States in the latter part of the 1800s, along with remarkable economic expansion, increased the need for legal services. The educational opportunities for those wishing to become lawyers were limited because the number of apprenticeships was inadequate, and, in any case, apprenticeships were generally not open to immigrants. Law schools became more important in this context, particularly in the 1920s when states began to consider the licensing of lawyers. At the beginning of that decade, no jurisdiction in the country required anything more than an apprenticeship to practice law, but by its end, all jurisdictions required lawyers to pass examinations (bar exams) before they could practice law. The number of law schools was increasing and they provided the best preparation for that exam.

Legal Services and Business and Industry
The end of the nineteenth century and the early years of the twentieth century were times of great economic expansion in the United States. A group known as Progressives, among them many lawyers, was disturbed by the negative effects of industrial development. The Progressives called for debate about the divisions between business practices and professionalism. The industrial society, they said, appeared to be exploiting laborers, putting great wealth in the hands of a few, exposing the public to dangers and harm, and corrupting the legislative and regulatory processes. Other lawyers defended corporations. Lawyers battled each other to define the proper behavior of business and industry.

State legislatures and Congress passed numerous regulatory and antitrust laws. One result was the development of law firms, efficiency-oriented associations of

Lawyer and future president Abraham Lincoln circa 1850s.

See also:
Arbitration; Product Liability; Regulation of Business and Industry.

lawyers whose operations reflected those of the businesses they served. As lawyers began working for and within big corporations, they aspired to the salaries and prestige of corporate executives. Lawyers began to specialize; each lawyer in a firm was encouraged to develop a field of expertise. Additionally, law firms adopted more businesslike modes of management. Law firms started advertising their services, something previously deemed unprofessional. They assumed top-down styles of control, with young associates required to work long hours under strict supervision on manageable parts of cases. Although the number of lawyers in private practice dwindled, the total number of lawyers swelled, and those in some firms ranked among the highest paid professionals in the United States.

Corporate lawyers searching through patent records in Washington, D.C. (undated).

Legal Services and U.S. Society

As the nature of law firms changed, so did the clientele. In the first half of the twentieth century, more than half of legal services were performed on behalf of individuals. By the 1970s less than 20 percent of legal services were devoted to individuals or to personal problems. Specialized lawyers who served corporate clients performed all other services. Research in 1977, for instance, pointed out that one-third of the population had never used a lawyer and those who did averaged little more than two visits in a lifetime. With the profession becoming so closely aligned with the upper class and big money, suspicions similar to those of the Progressive Era resurfaced. Critics were especially vocal in the 1980s. They asked if corporate thinking had corrupted traditional modes of practice and if the profession had abandoned the

Academic year	Total degrees conferred	Men	Women	Academic year	Total degrees conferred	Men	Women
			Law Degrees: Total and by Sex 1955 to 2000				
1955–1956	8,262	7,974	288	1981–1982	35,991	23,965	12,026
1957–1958	9,394	9,122	272	1982–1983	36,853	23,550	13,303
1959–1960	9,240	9,010	230	1983–1984	37,012	23,382	13,630
1961–1962	9,364	9,091	273	1984–1985	37,491	23,070	14,421
1963–1964	10,679	10,372	307	1985–1986	35,844	21,874	13,970
1965–1966	13,246	12,776	470	1986–1987	36,056	21,561	14,495
1967–1968	16,454	15,805	649	1987–1988	35,397	21,067	14,330
1969–1970	14,916	14,115	801	1988–1989	35,634	21,069	14,565
1970–1971	17,421	16,181	1,240	1989–1990	36,485	21,079	15,406
1971–1972	21,764	20,266	1,498	1990–1991	37,945	21,643	16,302
1972–1973	27,205	25,037	2,168	1991–1992	38,848	22,260	16,588
1973–1974	29,326	25,986	3,340	1992–1993	40,302	23,182	17,120
1974–1975	29,296	24,881	4,415	1993–1994	40,044	22,826	17,218
1975–1976	32,293	26,085	6,208	1994–1995	39,349	22,592	16,757
1976–1977	34,104	26,447	7,657	1995–1996	39,828	22,508	17,320
1977–1978	34,402	25,457	8,945	1996–1997	40,079	22,548	17,531
1978–1979	35,206	25,180	10,026	1997–1998	39,331	21,876	17,455
1979–1980	35,647	24,893	10,754	1998–1999	39,167	21,628	17,539
1980–1981	36,331	24,563	11,768	1999–2000	38,152	20,638	17,514

Note: Prior to 1970, data are available only in two-year periods.
Source: U.S. Department of Education, National Center for Education Statistics, *Higher Education General Information Survey*, 2001.

sanctity of the individual lawyer–client relationship or compromised personal ethics in its zeal for bureaucratic accountability.

Issues of equity challenged the legal profession from its beginning. Women, for example, were not allowed to enter the profession until 1870. Some professional organizations barred women from membership as late as 1937 and some law schools did not admit women until 1972. Similarly, blacks were not allowed in the American Bar Association until 1943 and were excluded from many law schools well into the 1950s.

Although access to the law—both for legal help and to the profession itself—has not always been open to everyone, the theoretical intent of the law is that it be administered fairly, regardless of a person's circumstances. The profession helps those who cannot afford legal representation in two ways: through volunteer services and with public defenders.

Associations of lawyers recommend that practitioners spend some of their time providing services to the disadvantaged at little or no cost—the charitable obligation known as *pro bono publico*. When it appeared that

lawyers' provision of pro bono services failed to fulfill the need, the courts took action. In 1938 the Supreme Court ruled that all persons had a constitutional right to legal defense in federal criminal cases. In 1963 that right was extended to state court felonies and nine years later to those accused

Careers in Legal Services

No professional training offers a more varied choice of employment than a law degree. Options range from private practice in a small town to chief counsel at the White House.

The law is attractive to idealists who want to advocate for social justice. Other lawyers work in the government as judges, prosecutors, public defenders, or as a part of agencies. Many politicians have a legal background as well; lawyers usually dominate both houses of Congress and most state legislatures. Some lawyers become law professors; others work in private practice, either alone or with associates; and others work in law firms.

Businesses use lawyers extensively. Some corporations purchase legal services from law firms; others have their own in-house legal staffs that handle issues related to finance, insurance, transportation, public utilities, commerce, real estate, manufacturing, personnel, and taxes.

Successful lawyers have the gift of decision making, the ability to understand the stakes involved, and can select the best path to follow. Essentially, lawyers' work consists of fitting a local narrative, or an account of the facts of a situation, with all the applicable rules, statutes, constitutional provisions, legal writings, and decisions to create a plausible legal narrative that will be accepted by judge and jury.

Discussing evidence with a witness in open court.

of misdemeanors punishable by six months' imprisonment.

States established salaried public defender programs to handle this work and some courts appointed private counsel when public defenders were not available. Legal aid societies were established to help poor clients with civil matters. The problem of poor clients being well represented, though, remains central to the profession. The legal profession still appears to serve some parts of society better than others. Legal services vary greatly in quality and quantity, especially across income levels. In general, wealthier clients have access to the best legal services, whereas legal services are still virtually unknown to other parts of society.

The legal profession has never been more prominent or more prosperous, more prevalent or more influential. It remains essential to American society both because of its role as interpreter and protector of the laws of the land and because it is the intended guardian of those who can take advantage of, as well as those who are subjected to, the laws of the land.

Further Reading

Cantor, Norman F. *Imagining the Law: Common Law and the Foundations of the American Legal System.* New York: HarperCollins, 1997.

Chroust, Anton-Hermann. *The Rise of the Legal Profession in America.* Norman: University of Oklahoma Press, 1965.

Friedman, Lawrence Meir. *American Law in the Twentieth Century.* New Haven, Conn.: Yale University Press, 2002.

Grossman, George S. *The Spirit of American Law.* Boulder, Colo.: Westview Press, 2000.

Kelly, Michael J. *Lives of Lawyers.* Ann Arbor: University of Michigan Press, 1994.

—*Karen Ehrle*

Levi Strauss & Co.

Since their invention in the nineteenth century, blue jeans have held sway as an emblem of American casual dress. Although many companies around the world now manufacture jeans, the durable pants are still associated with the company that invented them—Levi Strauss.

Although blue jeans were invented in the United States, they are made from denim, a durable, twilled fabric that originally came from Europe. The word *denim* derives from the name of a French material, *serge de Nîmes*. The word *jeans* comes from Genoa, Italy, its usage reflecting the fact that sailors from Genoa often wore clothes made of denim.

The inventor of blue jeans, Levi Strauss (1829–1902), was himself an import. Born Loeb Strauss in Buttenheim, now in southern Germany, Strauss was the son of a dry-goods peddler. In 1847 he traveled to New York, joining two of his older brothers who had already emigrated, and he and his brothers opened a dry-goods business. In 1853 Strauss traveled to San Francisco to serve as the west coast outlet for his family's business.

One particular clothing problem for the miners was pockets, which easily tore away from their jeans. A Nevada tailor named Jacob Davis had the idea of using metal rivets (fasteners) to hold the pockets and the jeans together firmly. Davis did not have enough money to patent his idea but suggested it to Strauss, and in 1873 they received the patent together, with Davis becoming a partner in Strauss's business. The copper-riveted, four-pocket "waist overalls" they produced were the first blue jeans.

Demand for the pants rose rapidly, enabling Strauss to open a factory and, by 1890, to incorporate his business. At the turn of the century, his blue jeans were no stylish accessory; they were work clothes, worn by miners, farmers, ranchers, and lumberjacks. Until the 1930s most city people would have seen blue jeans only while traveling in rural areas or perhaps at Wild West shows like the ones produced by Buffalo Bill Cody. During the Great Depression, however, the market for blue jeans expanded as people with little money bought the sturdiest clothes they could find. At the same time, some hard-pressed cattle ranchers turned to dude ranching, providing inexpensive but exotic holiday retreats for city people eager to experience something of the old West. Hollywood studios had already begun making Western movies, and the cowboy look became fashionable. Capitalizing on the trend, Levi Strauss & Co. began featuring cowboys in its advertisements for its jeans.

With the outbreak of World War II, the U.S. government placed restrictions on the amount of cotton that could be sold for nonmilitary use. Levi Strauss & Co.

See also:
Advertising; Brand Names;
Business Practice.

*Levi Strauss in
an undated portrait.*

changed the design of its jeans to use less material. Soldiers, many of whom came from rural areas, wore their jeans when off duty. As women increasingly turned to work in factories during the war, they also turned to wearing blue jeans.

Until mid-century, Levi Strauss & Co. had faced little competition in the market for blue jeans. Its patent for copper-riveted pockets, and its long history of strong sales in the western states, had kept competition largely at bay. By the end of the war, however, several new jeans companies had appeared, including Wrangler and Lee. In response, Levi Strauss & Co. began to refocus its marketing strategy in an effort to reach new buyers in a broad, national market. The company sought to take account of attitudinal changes emerging at the time, especially among young people.

In the 1950s blue jeans became a symbol. The image of casual roughness represented by blue jeans contrasted with contemporary images of adult propriety and authority. Actors like James Dean and Marlon Brando—wearing blue jeans with a defiant swagger in *Rebel without a Cause* (1955) and *The Wild One* (1954)—stood in contrast to the man in the gray flannel suit and students who always did their homework. Elvis Presley wore blue jeans in his hit film *Jailhouse Rock* (1957), underscoring the suggestion of sex appeal already associated with tight, low-slung jeans. Some schools banned the wearing of blue jeans, no doubt adding to their appeal. In this context, Levi Strauss & Co. responded effectively, emphasizing youthful rebelliousness in its advertisements. Similarly, in the 1960s, Levi Strauss & Co. advertisements featured rock groups like the Jefferson Airplane and Paul Revere and the Raiders. Once a basic necessity for hardworking miners and farmers, Levis® had become the jeans of choice for hip young men and women, and those who wished to think of themselves as hip and young.

The company always had been known for its liberal, forward-thinking orientation. Levi Strauss himself contributed generously to Roman Catholic, Protestant, and Jewish charities. The company was among the first in the garment manufacturing industry to racially integrate its workforce, to offer bonuses to garment workers, and to promote Hispanic workers to management positions. It was also an early leader in establishing AIDS support groups (1983); in offering full medical benefits to the unmarried partners of its employees (1992); and in adopting worldwide standards for all its contractors regarding wages, hours, working conditions, and environmental issues (1993). In 2000 *Fortune* magazine named Levi Strauss & Co. the second-best company in America for minority employees.

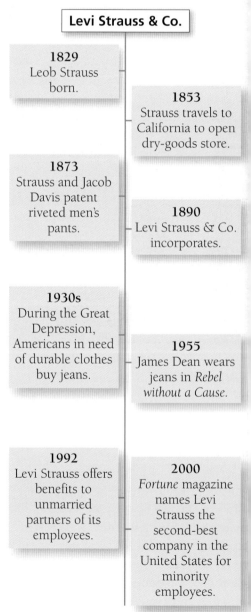

Levi Strauss & Co.

1829 Leob Strauss born.

1853 Strauss travels to California to open dry-goods store.

1873 Strauss and Jacob Davis patent riveted men's pants.

1890 Levi Strauss & Co. incorporates.

1930s During the Great Depression, Americans in need of durable clothes buy jeans.

1955 James Dean wears jeans in *Rebel without a Cause.*

1992 Levi Strauss offers benefits to unmarried partners of its employees.

2000 *Fortune* magazine names Levi Strauss the second-best company in the United States for minority employees.

In 2003 a model wears Levi Strauss & Co.'s Type 1™ jeans and jacket as part of the company's anniversary ad campaign titled "Bold since 1853."

Levi Strauss & Co. has responded nimbly to emerging trends throughout its history, distinguishing itself also by adopting forward-looking business practices. It lost market share in the 1980s as new designer jeans proliferated in a market cluttered with prestressed jeans, ripped jeans, recycled jeans, and painted jeans. At the same time, demand for vintage Levis® grew in Japan and elsewhere around the world, where the Levi Strauss name retained a special value among people fascinated by casual and provocative American styles.

Levi Strauss & Co. has also continued to respond nimbly in its domestic market, expanding its product line to include shirts, khaki slacks, dress slacks, jackets, and accessories for men and women.

Further Reading

Downey, Lynn. *This Is a Pair of Levi's Jeans: The Official History of the Levi's Brand.* Corte Madera, Calif.: Gingko Press, 1995.

Steenwyk, Elizabeth Van. *Levi Strauss: The Blue Jeans Man.* New York: Walker & Co., 1998.

—*Lisa Magloff*

Levitt, William

1907–1994
Creator of Levittowns

William Levitt is considered the father of the modern suburb. As the driving force behind Levitt and Sons, the multimillion-dollar construction company formed in 1929 by Abe Levitt and his sons William and Alfred, William Levitt pioneered the mass production of houses, enabling unprecedented numbers of Americans to own their own homes.

The Early Years

Levitt was born in Brooklyn, New York, in 1907. He attended New York University for three years before he quit, explaining that he "got itchy" to make money. After trying his hand at several jobs, including a stint in his father's law firm, he and his father decided to build a house on a piece of Long Island property they had not been able to sell. Shortly thereafter, Alfred also quit NYU and drew the plans for this first endeavor of Levitt and Sons. When that first house sold at a profit, the business was launched.

With Alfred designing and Bill handling the selling and organizing, Levitt and Sons sold 600 houses over the next four years. In 1934 the company built Strathmore-at-Manhasset, an upscale development of 200 homes on Long Island's north shore. Over the next seven years, the firm built 2,000 more houses.

In the early 1940s the Levitt brothers began their first experiment in mass producing houses near Norfolk, Virginia. The result was a village of shacklike houses that were a financial flop. They were more successful, however, in mass producing housing for members of the U.S. Navy in Norfolk. That project convinced them that houses could indeed be profitably mass-produced.

The business was put on hold in 1943, when Bill Levitt joined the Seabees, a construction battalion of the Civil Engineer Corps of the U.S. Navy. After serving as a lieutenant for two years, Levitt left the service and Levitt and Sons picked up where it left off. "The dice were loaded," Levitt said of this time. "The market was there and the government was ready with the backing. How could we lose?"

Levittown

Although Levitt built many housing developments, he is best known for Levittown, New York, a suburb on Long Island just 25 miles east of Manhattan. He later built Levittowns in New Jersey and Pennsylvania. In Levittown, New York, on land that used to be potato fields, the template for his housing revolution took form.

In 1947, when Levitt broke ground on Levittown, most builders completed an average of four houses per year. Levitt and Sons, however, completed 30 a day. Levitt liked to compare his company to General Motors,

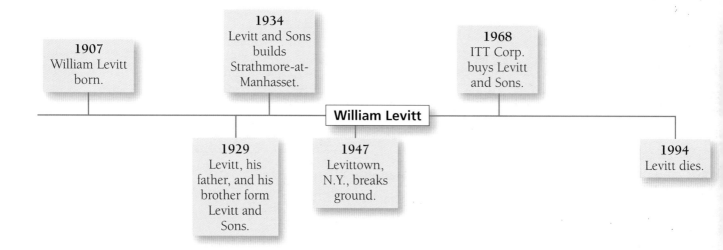

1907
William Levitt born.

1934
Levitt and Sons builds Strathmore-at-Manhasset.

1968
ITT Corp. buys Levitt and Sons.

William Levitt

1929
Levitt, his father, and his brother form Levitt and Sons.

1947
Levittown, N.Y., breaks ground.

1994
Levitt dies.

stating, "We channel labor and materials to a stationary outdoor assembly line instead of bringing them together inside a factory."

The mass production began at Levitt's central warehouse, where lumber was pre-cut to size, plumbing fixtures were assembled, staircases were prefabricated, and most of the building materials for each house, including bricks, shingles and copper tubing, were bundled together. Then the bundles were placed at each building site, every 60 feet, over newly laid streets.

Levitt had broken down the construction process into 27 distinct operations, with each performed by a crew trained for its specific task. In rapid succession these crews—none of which were union—trenched the sites, poured foundations, laid bricks, raised studs, nailed lathe, sheathed, and shingled. Levitt had a crew for tiling, another for installing appliances, and even a separate crew for each paint color.

In addition to the speed achieved by this specialization, much of Levitt and Sons' profitability came from buying supplies direct from manufacturers, a practice new to the building industry at that time. Levitt did not stop at buying appliances, piping, and bricks direct; he bought whole timber stands and a sawmill in Oregon to ensure a steady supply

of lumber. He also used many labor-saving devices, for example, paint sprayers, that were banned by the building unions.

These Levitt homes, which sat on one-seventh-acre lots, sold for $7,990, a price that allowed for about $1,000 profit. They were 750-square-foot homes with two bedrooms, a living room, a kitchen, an unfinished second floor and no garage. Included were a stove, refrigerator, washing machine, and built-in

William Levitt in his office in 1961.

The house at 3626 Regent Lane, in Levittown, New York, in 1958.

Levittown, New York.

television; later models included amenities like garages. Fifty years later, those same houses were selling for about $155,000.

Levitt and Sons eventually built 17,000 houses in Levittown. However, these houses, like the millions of other mass-produced houses built across the country during the postwar years, would never have been possible without government-backed loans. During World War II the building industry had stagnated, with both labor and materials in short supply. After the war, the Federal Housing Administration (FHA) determined that the United States needed 5,000,000 more houses and paved the way for developers by making available billions of dollars in credit. The FHA guaranteed the loans that banks made to builders and also federally insured the buyers' mortgages. By 1950 the purchase terms on low-cost houses were nearly as easy as renting: 5 percent down and 30 years to pay; for veterans, down payment was not required. Monthly payments on a Levitt home, for example, could be as low as $56 per month.

The Levitts grew rich building cheap houses, but that rising tide was not eternal for Bill Levitt. In 1968, after building approximately 140,000 houses, Levitt and Sons was sold to ITT Corp. for $92 million in stock, most of which went to Levitt. He spent lavishly on yachts and mansions and used the stock as collateral to build subdivisions in Iran, Venezuela, and Nigeria. By 1972 the ITT stock had lost 90 percent of its value and Levitt was millions of dollars in debt. He died in Manhasset, New York, in 1994.

Levitt helped instigate the tremendous demographic shift in the United States from city to suburb. For returning servicemen living with relatives in crammed city apartments, the tiny houses were grand. For the wage-earner of modest means, Levitt put the American dream of owning a home within reach. As Levitt's methods were copied by builders across the country, the modern suburb became a common feature of the American landscape.

Further Reading

Kelly, Barbara M. *Expanding the American Dream: Building and Rebuilding Levittown.* New York: State University of New York Press, 1993.
"Up from the Potato Fields." *Time,* 3 July 1950, 67–72.

—*Barbara Gerber*

Lewis, Reginald

1942–1993
Entrepreneur

Before his death at the age of 50, Reginald Lewis was the CEO of the largest black-owned business in the country, TLC Beatrice, and had created a personal fortune estimated at $400 million. The attitude that produced his success was in evidence at age six when he overheard his grandparents talking about the limited opportunities for blacks in the United States. They wondered if circumstances would be different for their grandson. "Yeah," piped up young Reginald, "why should white guys have all the fun?"

Lewis was born in 1942 in East Baltimore, Maryland, the only child of Clinton and Carolyn Cooper Lewis. When his parents divorced, his mother and five-year-old Reginald moved into the maternal grandparents' house. At age 10 Lewis got his first job delivering an African American newspaper. Displaying early his aggressive business instincts, Lewis increased the route from 10 customers to 100. While attending the all-black Dunbar High School in East Baltimore, Lewis earned the nickname "Bullet Lewis" for the powerful passes he threw for the football team. He also excelled in baseball and basketball and held several part-time jobs. In this period he told a friend that his goal was to be the richest black man in the country.

Lewis worked hard everywhere but in the classroom; nevertheless, he got a football scholarship to Virginia State College. However, Lewis's height of 5'10" relegated him to third-string quarterback duties; he gave up the scholarship and juggled work, school, and fun for the remainder of his undergraduate years, graduating in 1965.

Lewis wanted to go to Harvard Law School, but his grades, especially from the first year when he was playing football, were not good enough. His solution was a summer school program at Harvard designed to interest black students in the study of law. That the program was meant only for undergraduates or that Virginia State had already selected its candidates did not matter to Lewis. He gathered testimonials from professors, got himself added to the list, and ultimately was selected by Harvard to participate. Even though the summer program was designed specifically to not circumvent the Harvard Law School admission process, Lewis did just that by making such important contributions each day that he could not be ignored. By the end of the summer, he had managed to be admitted to Harvard Law School before he formally applied.

Upon graduation in 1968 Lewis began work with the New York firm of Paul,

See also:
Small Business Administration; Venture Capital.

TLC Beatrice CEO Reginald Lewis.

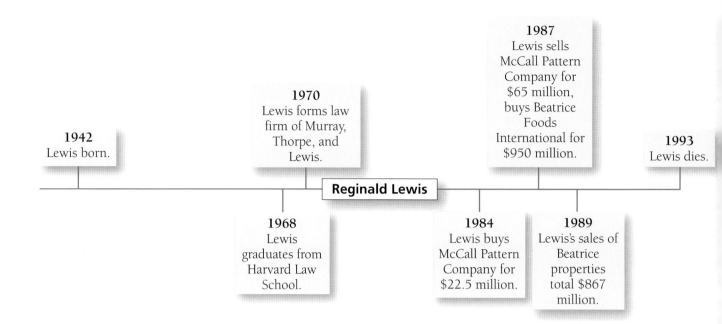

1942
Lewis born.

1968
Lewis graduates from Harvard Law School.

1970
Lewis forms law firm of Murray, Thorpe, and Lewis.

Reginald Lewis

1984
Lewis buys McCall Pattern Company for $22.5 million.

1987
Lewis sells McCall Pattern Company for $65 million, buys Beatrice Foods International for $950 million.

1989
Lewis's sales of Beatrice properties total $867 million.

1993
Lewis dies.

Weiss. In 1970 he formed Murray, Thorpe, and Lewis, a black-run law firm serving small businesses while also helping the Urban Coalition create housing for low- and moderate-income people. Lewis eventually bought out his partners. By 1972 the firm's prime source of revenue were so-called MESBICS, which were minority venture capital firms funded by corporations and the Small Business Administration. Lewis made many useful contacts through this work and also learned how to acquire a business through the use of debt financing.

Lewis developed a successful legal practice, but he felt being black forced him to prove himself again to each new client. He believed that real recognition would come only from the acquisition of a multimillion-dollar corporation. From 1975 to 1983 Lewis and his venture capital firm TLC (The Lewis Company) attempted several takeovers. Each attempt taught Lewis valuable lessons, which he applied in 1984 in the acquisition of McCall Pattern Company for $22.5 million, none of it Lewis's own money.

Under Lewis's leadership, income doubled in 1985 and again in 1986. In 1987 McCall was sold for $65 million, almost three times what Lewis had paid for it three years earlier. An original investor in TLC received a 90 to 1 return on the investment (calculation includes dividends).

In August of 1987, TLC won the right to purchase Beatrice Foods International for $950 million, the deal to be closed by December 1. While arranging the financing for this deal, Lewis made agreements to sell off units of Beatrice in Canada, Australia, and Spain for $340 million, thereby reducing the amount of the final price he needed to finance. He also had to overcome investor fears (caused by the huge decline in the Dow Jones stock index in October of that year) and master the complexities of international business taxation before the deal could be finalized, just one hour before the December 1 deadline.

Lewis was now the head of TLC Beatrice, the largest black-owned business in the United States, and the first with more than $1 billion in annual revenue. By 1989 he had sold Beatrice properties totaling $867 million, or 88 percent of the 1987 purchase price. This lowered the debt-to-equity ratio from 70 to 1 (when purchased) to 1.6 to 1. In 1990 the managers of a leaner, more efficient TLC Beatrice presented a plan to increase

[Reginald Lewis] is to me what Joe Louis is to me. What Jackie Robinson is to me. Regardless of race, color, or creed, we are all dealt a hand to play in this game of life. And believe me, Reg Lewis played the hell out of his hand.

—Bill Cosby in his eulogy to Reginald Lewis

operating income by an extraordinary 47 percent. CEO Lewis told them that goal was not ambitious enough. With his encouragement and determination, operating income was increased by 56 percent.

Reginald Lewis's determination carried him from a black, middle-class upbringing to the top of corporate America. His death from brain cancer in 1993 at the age of 50 leaves unanswered the question of just how much further he could have gone. Lewis had an extraordinary ability to set goals and to do whatever was required to achieve them. He did so by following three rules: do your homework, work hard, and have good people working for you.

The boy who did not study hard in high school became the man who did his homework so well that he amassed a personal fortune of $400 million. The Reginald Lewis International Law Center at Harvard University and Reginald Lewis Trailblazers Award of the Rainbow/PUSH Coalition are just two of the tangible testimonials to the remarkable rise of a black man whose determination is legendary.

Further Reading

Clarke, Caroline V. *Take a Lesson: Today's Black Achievers on How They Made It and What They Learned along the Way.* New York: John Wiley & Sons, 2001.

Graves, Earl G. *How to Succeed in Business without Being White: Straight Talk on Making It in America.* New York: HarperBusiness, 1997.

Lewis, Reginald F., and Blair S. Walker. *"Why Should White Guys Have All The Fun?": How Reginald Lewis Created a Billion-Dollar Business Empire.* New York: John Wiley & Sons, 1995.

—*Gary Baughn*

Carolyn E. Fugett, mother of the late Reginald Lewis, and Lewis's widow, Loida, are greeted by NAACP president Kweisi Mfume at a press conference in June 1999. The press conference was held to announce the creation of a $1 million endowment by the Reginald F. Lewis Family and Foundation for the NAACP Reginald F. Lewis Youth Entrepreneurial Institute.

Liability

Liability refers to the legal responsibility that a company (or individual) brings upon itself by harming another party or violating a state or federal law. Actions that incur liability include any of a wide range of wrongdoings, from failing to perform a contractual obligation to causing an injury through the inadequacy of a product or service to destroying an entire ecosystem by accident or irresponsible waste management. Generally, a party who is found liable for a harm to another party pays monetary damages. If the party has incurred civil or criminal liability by violating a state or federal statute, that party may be subject to fines or imprisonment.

The principle of liability in law and public policy provides compensation to wronged parties and serves as a form of deterrence against similar violations in the future. The possibility of a liability lawsuit is one way of guaranteeing that businesses meet their contractual obligations, as well as do everything in their power to make their products, services, workplaces, and manufacturing processes comply with public health and safety standards.

U.S. liability law underwent sweeping reforms in the twentieth century. After World War II, the country's relative wealth and stability allowed citizens to focus on health and safety issues. Beginning in the late 1950s and early 1960s, consumer advocates like Ralph Nader warned the public of the environmental, health, and safety risks posed by big business and industry. Slowly legislators and the courts found better ways to hold companies accountable for defective products and careless practices that threatened citizens' health and livelihood.

In the gallery of the Mississippi state senate, activists watch lawmakers debate tort reform in 2002.

Although these trends appear to be completely positive, much debate has occurred about whether they are truly beneficial to the American public. To better understand the conflicting arguments, the differences and tensions between three main areas of liability law—contractual, tort, and statutory liability—must first be defined.

Contractual Liability

Remarkably little has changed in contractual liability law since the seventeenth century, when the principles of contract law were first developed in England. A contract is a binding promise between two parties. It may be verbal or written and establishes that the two parties have a duty to one another to fulfill the agreed-upon terms. When that duty is not fulfilled by either party, a breach of the contract occurs, and the breaching party is liable for compensatory damages, which make the wronged party "whole" based on the terms of the contract. The breaching party is required to pay the injured party for all financial loss resulting from the breach of contract.

Although market forces eventually eliminate companies that earn a reputation for not following through on their promises, common law courts applying commercial law principles understood that for companies to take necessary risks, they needed more immediate assurance that their contractual agreements would be enforced. Indeed, in twenty-first-century business and industry, individuals, companies, and governments have formed such complex dependencies upon one another for goods and services that legally enforceable contracts are essential to the health of the economy. Applying the principle of liability is essential to the enforcement of contracts. Contractual liability compensates parties who suffer economic loss through breach of contract, and it provides some deterrence to the breaching of contracts.

Tort and Statutory Liability

Under the area of law called torts, or civil wrongs, a party may be found liable for

Tort Actions Commenced and Pending 1996 to 1999				
YEAR	1996	1997	1998	1999
COMMENCED Tort Actions	67,029	52,710	52,218	39,785
PENDING Tort Actions	66,823	72,250	63,683	84,073

Note: Figures compiled from U.S. district courts.
Source: U.S. Bureau of the Census, Statistical Abstract of the United States, 2001.

causing injury to an individual's person or property. Before the reform that began in the late 1950s and 1960s, tort law was distinct from contract law because it covered interactions between parties where no express or implied contract was present—for example, traffic accidents and assaults. However, tort reformers recognized that in some consensual interactions where an express or implied contract was present, as between buyer and seller, employer and employee, and hospital and patient, the law of contracts was inadequate because the parties' bargaining power was unequal. Consumers did not necessarily understand or have the power to change buyer–seller agreements created by the seller, just as individuals did not have the power to insist that employers and hospitals assume liability for unsafe conditions or risky or incompetently performed procedures.

Hence, changes in tort law reflected a desire to address some of these inequities between individuals and big business. Tort reform sought to place power in the hands of consumers, employees, patients, and similar individuals who otherwise had no recourse if they were injured—limited as they were by contract terms that absolved larger parties of any and all liability. Indeed, in cases where an individual was seen as having no ability to negotiate the terms of the contract, courts began to call the contracts "contracts of adhesion" and refused to enforce their unfair terms.

This thinking paved the way to other important developments that marked this era of reform. Previous tort cases had been based on proving either the defendant's intentional misconduct or negligence; now individuals and companies could be found

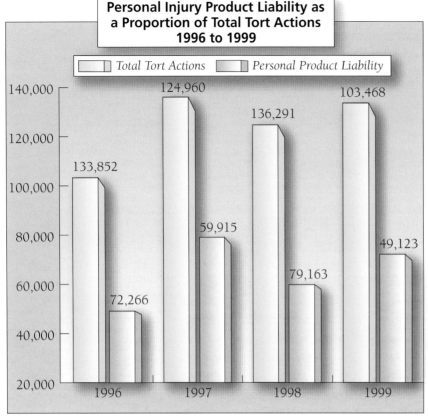

Personal Injury Product Liability as a Proportion of Total Tort Actions 1996 to 1999

Total Tort Actions · Personal Product Liability

- 1996: 133,852 / 72,266
- 1997: 124,960 / 59,915
- 1998: 136,291 / 79,163
- 1999: 103,468 / 49,123

Note: Figures are compiled from U.S. district courts.
Source: U.S. Bureau of the Census, *Statistical Abstract of the United States,* 2001.

to have "strict" liability for injury to persons or property; thus intention or negligence were no longer the issues in many lawsuits. Companies could be held responsible for selling a product or service that caused harm to an individual or for causing indirect harm through manufacturing processes, for example, injuries to a worker by factory machinery or harmful toxins spewed into the environment by manufacturing processes.

The damages assessed became higher than ever. In addition to compensatory damages, successful tort plaintiffs could be awarded punitive damages, which serve to punish the wrongdoer. Juries began awarding such high punitive damages that businesses were forced to change their procedures.

Hand in hand with tort reform came the rapid passage of state and federal statutes that required businesses and industries to meet stricter health and safety standards. In addition to adding to the powers of existing organizations like the

Food and Drug Administration (FDA), the government created new agencies like the Environmental Protection Agency (EPA) and the Occupational Safety and Health Administration (OSHA) to oversee and enforce the newly enacted regulations.

These tort and statutory reforms are now firmly entrenched in the U.S. legal system, but one cannot overestimate the extent to which they have transformed American life. At the beginning of the twenty-first century, America's homes, workplaces, hospitals, and public spaces are safer than ever, and businesses are paying strict attention to public health and the environment. America's health and safety standards have, in fact, become a model for other countries. The 2000 Academy Award–winning film *Erin Brockovich* celebrated liability principles at their best, telling the story of the famous class-action suit that awarded $333 million to residents of Hinkley, California, where groundwater had been knowingly polluted with a cancer-causing chemical by Pacific Gas and Electric.

Tort Reform and Its Critics
Americans are inspired by such accounts of big business brought to its knees by individuals asserting their rights. However, some critics claim that tort and statutory reform primarily benefit not the American people in general, but rather lawyers and plaintiffs who go after the deep pockets of large companies whenever possible, seeking a high punitive damage award—even when a liability claim is frivolous at best. Big business and industry are at the forefront of calls for further reform that would reduce high litigation fees, punitive damages, and liability insurance premiums.

Critics of the current system argue that liability principles are unfairly biased against large companies. For instance, under current law, a large company that is found only partly liable for an injury may be required to pay full damages if the other liable parties are unable to pay their share (often because of bankruptcy). In "successor" liability cases, a company that has

The legal system in the United States has been widely criticized for being too costly, inefficient and ineffective in administering fair awards. In particular, the contemporary tort system in the U.S. has deteriorated because of perverse incentives that lead to skyrocketing costs. Because of our current third party insurance system, and its pain and suffering damage recoveries that sustain contingency fee litigation, perverse incentives and standards have developed that drive up the cost of the tort system. In the auto insurance field, these incentives have produced a system riddled with fraud and abuse, and along with the tort system as a whole, they have generated costly, unnecessary and fraudulent medical claims. All of these problems add up to a huge economic burden for individuals, businesses, and government. According to a recent study by the actuarial firm Tillinghast-Towers Perrin, 1994 tort costs are up 125 percent from the 1984 level.

The economic consequences of such heavy tort costs are considerable. First, individuals suffer directly by having less disposable income than they would otherwise due to higher premiums for automobile and other forms of insurance. Second, individuals suffer indirectly when businesses, forced to pay higher premiums for product liability and other forms of insurance, raise their prices on goods and services. Third, when businesses have to charge higher prices, they do less business than they would otherwise, which in turn slows down job expansion and economic growth. Individuals bear the brunt of this economic slowdown in the form of lower wages and fewer jobs. Finally, increasing litigiousness discourages businesses and individuals from taking risks, which means that fewer new products are brought to market and new technologies are either delayed or forgone altogether.

Individuals living and working in urban areas are particularly affected by the high costs of the tort system, because cities and other densely populated areas have experienced an even greater increase in the tort costs. In New York City, for instance, municipal litigation costs increased 187 percent between 1984 and 1994, and such costs are increasing at a 12 percent annual rate thus far in the 1990s. In addition, municipal residents pay relatively more in auto insurance and other tort-related costs, thereby adding to the economic burdens of urban residents. In the current environment of fiscal responsibility and taxpayer flight from cities, urban governments and residents can ill-afford to allocate large portions of their budgets to litigation costs.

One of the driving forces behind tort costs is insurance fraud and exaggeration. To gauge the extent to which claims of outright fraud are responsible for rapid increases in health and auto insurance premiums, the Federal Bureau of Investigation (FBI) began an investigation of staged automobile accidents. The results of this inquiry led FBI Director Louis Freeh to estimate that "[e]very American household is burdened with more than $200 annually in additional insurance premiums to make up for this type of fraud. . . ."

[Tort reform has] the potential to improve the overall quality of the American legal system. Not only would the three reforms offer injured parties more choices in seeking redress, but rewards would be administered more efficiently and fairly. . . .

The value of these reforms goes beyond mere dollar savings. In all likelihood, lives would be saved as a restructured auto insurance system would encourage the production of safer vehicles. All individuals who switched to auto-choice would likely see further insurance discounts for driving safer vehicles. More generally, these reforms would help correct the current system's tendency to discourage the introduction of new products and technologies.

As indicated, these proposals would generate highly progressive savings, lower unacceptably high transaction costs, enhance the rights and choices available to injured parties, and eliminate the incentives for fraud and misconduct that permeate today's tort system. For these reasons, one of the greatest virtues of these proposals is their potential to reestablish the esteem in which many Americans hold the legal system. As the tort system affects all Americans in both direct and indirect ways, tort reform can play a critically-needed role in halting the precipitous, if understandable, decline in respect for the U.S. legal system

—Joint Economic Committee, *Improving the American Legal System:*
The Economic Benefits of Tort Reform, 1996

bought the assets of another company and continued to produce the exact product may be found liable for an injury caused by the original company's product.

The debate over the fairness of current liability policies extends to regulatory agencies. For instance, in its effort to clean up toxic waste dumps, the EPA has been criticized for its practice of holding all companies that used a dump equally liable for its cleanup costs—even in cases where determining how much each company contributed to the toxicity of the site, if at all, is difficult or impossible. Businesses and industries are further frustrated by tort and statutory laws that work against one

For the last 16 years, the tobacco, pharmaceutical, auto, oil, chemical, and health care industries, and their insurers, have fought to limit peoples' rights to sue and to further limit their own liability for the damages they cause innocent victims. Aimed in the direction of Congress and the state legislatures, this coalition of insurance companies and corporate defendants' lobbies has relied on misinformation and anecdotal evidence to attack and destroy decades of slow but careful progress made by state court after state court respecting the physical integrity of human beings against harm. This wrongdoers coalition is out to convince lawmakers to view this progressive evolution not as a source of national pride, or as a source of public recognition that the weak and the defenseless sometimes get justice, but rather as a source of shame, as a source of economic destructiveness, as something that should be stopped.

The current administration has signed into law several pieces of "tort deform" legislation that takes away the rights of injured consumers to sue the perpetrators of their harm. . . . The civil justice system provides our society with its moral and ethical fiber. When the rights of injured consumers are vindicated in court, our society benefits in countless ways: by compensating injured victims and shattered families for unspeakable losses (and saving taxpayers from having to assist them); by preventing future injuries by removing dangerous products and practices from the marketplace and spurring safety innovation; by educating the public to unnecessary and unacceptable risks associated with some products and services through disclosure of facts discovered during trial; and by providing authoritative judicial forums for the ethical growth of law where the responsibility of perpetrators of trauma and disease can be established. This authoritative expansion of respect for human life serves to distinguish our country from most other nations.

The tort deform legislation that has been proposed in Congress and in state legislatures around the country over the last 15 years undermines each of these functions. Under tort deform, the most severely injured or disease-afflicted Americans — seniors in nursing homes, quadriplegic workers or brain-damaged children who suffer most and suffer for a lifetime — are prohibited from obtaining fair compensation for their injuries and are unable to hold the perpetrators of their harm accountable. Indeed, "tort deform" laws take away the rights of 99 percent of the people who live in this country, while letting a handful of corporations escape accountability for reckless misconduct that causes injury and death. They are also unfair to the well-behaved companies. Business wrongdoers should be held responsible fully for their damage to innocent people. When courts make these defendants accountable for their damage, the companies have a greater incentive to produce safer products or conditions. This is the lesson of legal history.

Tort deforms are also a direct interference with the independence of the civil justice system, often the only place where an individual can effectively challenge raw corporate and financial power. Judges and jurors are free from the influence of corporate lobbyists, who wine and dine regulators and use their influence to weaken regulations, and the lure of the corporate revolving door. Tort deforms tie the hands of our courts — both judges and juries — by legislators who never see, hear or evaluate the evidence in each specific case, thus undermining our uniquely individualized system of justice. . . .

Tort deforms make it difficult or impossible for American consumers who suffer death, brain injury, amputation, paralysis, quadriplegia, cancer and other devastating injuries at the hands of corporate wrongdoers, to be fully compensated for their harm. They increase the many obstacles faced by consumers who are hurt by defective products, toxic chemicals and dangerous drugs, already face in bringing offenders to justice. Tort deform is nothing more than a bailout from liability and responsibility for corporations, including the largest and richest corporations in the world at the expense of all Americans. The tragic costs, human and economic, are borne by the wrongfully injured and their families, not by the wrongdoers themselves.

—Ralph Nader in excerpt from 2000 presidential campaign platform,
http://www.votenader.com/issues/tort_full.html (April 28, 2003)

another, as when successful tort lawsuits are brought against companies that have met the minimum standards of agencies like the FDA, EPA, and OSHA. Moreover, many regulatory agencies have been accused of actually aiding the companies they are supposed to regulate by softening their regulatory standards or acting slowly to enforce new legislation.

Perhaps the greatest concern is that the American public is, in fact, paying for the costs of tort and statutory reform. Rarely do companies simply absorb the financial losses associated with litigation, liability insurance, and the costs of meeting state and federal standards—rather they raise the price of goods and services. Americans may pay for high health and safety standards in ways that are less easy to gauge. Companies may forgo innovation, stick with less risky products and services, withdraw important goods and services from the market, and establish factories and plants in other countries with less stringent standards. The high cost of liability lawsuits may make American companies less competitive with other countries' businesses and industries, thus weakening the economic health of the United States as a whole.

Future Reforms

All of these concerns demand the attention of law and public policy makers, and critics point to proposed modifications in existing policies that would eliminate some of their unfairness and inefficiencies. Liability principles could be revised so lawyers and plaintiffs were encouraged to sue only those parties truly responsible for an injury, rather than targeting companies with deep pockets.

To discourage frivolous lawsuits, the United States might follow the lead of countries like the United Kingdom and require losing parties to pay the litigation costs and attorneys' fees of the prevailing party. Courts could place caps on punitive damages and encourage alternate forms of dispute resolution—mediation and arbitration, for example—that would decrease costs to defendants (as well as benefits to litigators). Regulatory agencies could be held more accountable for their own effectiveness and efficiency.

Even the most strident detractors do not argue for simply eliminating the tort and statutory reforms of the twentieth century. These reforms were born out of an idealistic vision of America as an economic leader that still protects its citizens. The question is whether the desire for the legal system and government to set high health and safety standards can be reconciled with the equally powerful desire for businesses to be allowed to function at the lowest cost possible. "The people's good is the highest law," said the Roman orator Cicero in the

Liability goes Hollywood; Julia Roberts stars in Erin Brockovich *(2000).*

Monitoring a toxic-waste site in 1993. Companies that improperly dispose of toxic waste can be held liable for the costs of cleanup.

first century B.C.E., reflecting the intentions of current liability law—but ignoring the complexities of deciding what policies will in fact work in the people's best interest.

Further Reading

Committee for Economic Development, Research and Policy Committee. *Who Should Be Liable? A Guide to Policy for Dealing with Risk.* New York: Committee for Economic Development, 1989.

Drivon, Laurence E., with Bob Schmidt. *The Civil War on Consumer Rights.* Berkeley, Calif.: Conari Press, 1990.

Hans, Valerie P. *Business on Trial: The Civil Jury and Corporate Responsibility.* New Haven, Conn.: Yale University Press, 2000.

Huber, Peter. *The Legal Revolution and Its Consequences.* New York: Basic Books, 1988.

Wills, Robert V. *Lawyers Are Killing America: A Trial Lawyer's Appeal for Genuine Tort Reform.* Santa Barbara, Calif.: Capra Press, 1990.

—*Andrea Troyer and John Troyer*

License

A license is a kind of contract that grants permission to manufacture, copy, distribute, sell, or use intellectual property including inventions, patents, trademarks, service marks, writings, music, artwork, films, and computer programs. A license agreement may involve payment of fees or royalties, but unlike contracts related to the sale of tangible goods, a license does not involve a sale of the property, but rather the sale of specific rights to the property. The owner of the property, the licensor, transfers some rights to the licensee while reserving others.

When an individual or a business purchases a computer program from a software company, for instance, the buyer becomes a licensee paying a licensor for the limited right to use the program on a computer. The buyer does not own the contents of the program in the sense that she can duplicate and sell it herself. Indeed, a buyer would most likely be in violation of the license agreement if she did so.

Licenses of intellectual property come in many forms, but all withhold some rights associated with their properties; if a license granted all rights, it would be a sales contract of the property and not a license. Licenses are always conditional. They explicitly state under what terms and conditions the intellectual property may be used or distributed by the licensee, often including specific time frames, quantities, and methods. They may assert that the property cannot be modified, transferred to another person or company, or used for performance, display, or resale. They usually guard against the removal of copyright or other proprietary notices, and they clearly identify the owner of the property and the federal or state government agencies having jurisdiction over the property rights. Often, licenses also include disclaimers and limitations of liability.

Why Are Licenses Important?

A company may profit from ownership of intellectual property by turning it into a tangible product and marketing it. Alternatively, it may allow another company to do so, usually for something in return, a royalty, for example. The latter method is where licenses come into play. A company will not profit from granting another company access to its intellectual property unless a license agreement is made, one that identifies the way in which the licensor will be compensated, as well as the specific rights granted to the licensee and retained or reserved by the licensor. Because the sale of intellectual property is now the biggest and fastest-growing industry in the United States—contributing hundreds of billions of dollars to

See also:
Contracts and Contract Law;
Copyright; E-Business;
Intellectual Property; Patent.

An elephant crushes pirated software CDs seized in anti-piracy raids. This press briefing was organized by India's National Association of Software and Services Companies in April 1999 in New Delhi.

the economy and comprising over 50 percent of U.S. exports—license agreements are essential in today's business world.

Why don't companies always create a tangible product and sell their intellectual property in that form? Because a license agreement is often more practical or inexpensive, allowing companies maximum profit in little time. For instance, a license agreement may allow a company to quickly expand both its product and geographic markets, as when a film company licenses rights to an overseas video company. Some products are simply marketed more effectively when combined with another product, as demonstrated by Microsoft licensing the Windows operating system to sellers of personal computers.

Licenses also allow companies to combine resources and share new technology without the complications of a joint venture or merger. Companies may have more control over the direction of the industry and their part in it through licenses, again demonstrated by Microsoft, which, through its license agreement with IBM in the 1980s, made itself essential to the computer industry. Software developers who wanted IBM's business wrote their programs for the Microsoft operating system; other hardware developers soon chose to license that operating system as well. Record labels are working intensely to create license agreements for downloadable music, hoping to benefit rather than lose from the rising demand for music distributed in digital format. Companies have to respond quickly to shifts in technology and the market, and one way to do so is by use of license agreements.

For these strategies to work, however, a body of law that recognizes intellectual property rights and is willing to enforce them must be in place or must be created. The U.S. legal system allows companies to pursue legal remedies when their rights or license agreements are violated. They may seek injunctive relief, which is a legal order to suspend the licensee's use or distribution of the product. If the licensee does not respond to the injunction,

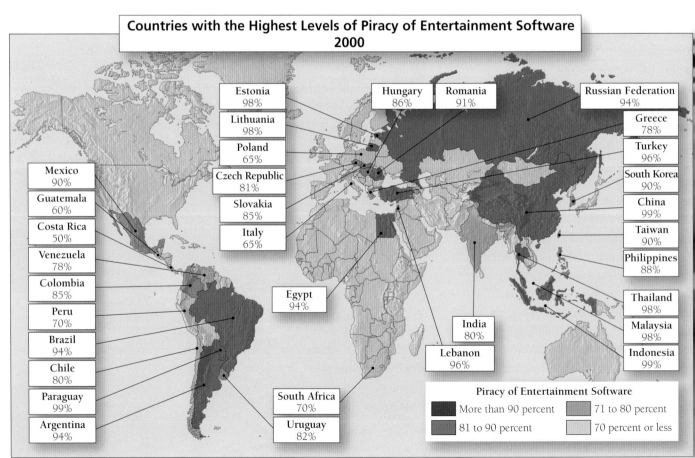

Countries with the Highest Levels of Piracy of Entertainment Software 2000

Estonia 98%
Lithuania 98%
Poland 65%
Czech Republic 81%
Slovakia 85%
Italy 65%

Hungary 86%
Romania 91%

Russian Federation 94%
Greece 78%
Turkey 96%
South Korea 90%
China 99%
Taiwan 90%
Philippines 88%
Thailand 98%
Malaysia 98%
Indonesia 99%

Mexico 90%
Guatemala 60%
Costa Rica 50%
Venezuela 78%
Colombia 85%
Peru 70%
Brazil 94%
Chile 80%
Paraguay 99%
Argentina 94%

Egypt 94%
India 80%
Lebanon 96%

South Africa 70%
Uruguay 82%

Piracy of Entertainment Software
More than 90 percent
81 to 90 percent
71 to 80 percent
70 percent or less

Source: International Intellectual Property Alliance.

he licensee may be held in contempt of court and subject to fines and imprisonment.

However, in countries like Brazil, India, Russia, South Korea, Taiwan, and Ukraine, intellectual property rights are not protected in the same way as in the United States. In these countries, sometimes called "free-riding countries," intellectual property is considered to be common property; anyone with the capability of copying and distributing intellectual property may do so without penalty. These countries' economies benefit from such policies because the companies located therein do not have to pay royalties or the costs of developing their own intellectual property—while U.S. companies lose an estimated $20 to $22 billion a year in potential profits. To minimize such losses, the United States has signed agreements with many countries that set uniform laws on intellectual property rights and license agreements. In addition, the United States imposes export restrictions and high tariffs on countries that fail to recognize and satisfactorily enforce intellectual property laws.

Licenses in the Information Age

Even within the United States, some dissatisfaction has been expressed with the legal system's governance of licenses. Information products and services now play such a large part in driving our economy that the industry is looking to the system for new laws that specifically accommodate their transactions, which often are much different in character from those related to manufactured goods. New guidelines for software and e-business licenses are especially crucial as these industries rely so heavily on licenses to define their transactions. For instance, in a software sale, the value of the sale is determined by the license terms; the value changes according to the number of copies that are allowed by the license: one or 1,000 or 10,000.

The legal system's enforcement of licenses has proven to be a primary concern as advances in technology make it easy and inexpensive to copy and distribute software illegally. Software companies are concerned about piracy, both at home and abroad; Web sites

---

An Open Letter to Hobbyists
(Excerpt)

Almost a year ago, Paul Allen and myself, expecting the [computer] hobby market to expand, hired Monte Davidoff and developed Altair BASIC. Though the initial work took only two months, the three of us have spent most of the last year documenting, improving and adding features to BASIC. Now we have 4K, 8K, EXTENDED, ROM and DISK BASIC. The value of the computer time we have used exceeds $40,000.

The feedback we have gotten from the hundreds of people who say they are using BASIC has all been positive. Two surprising things are apparent, however, (1) Most of these "users" never bought BASIC (less than 10% of all Altair owners have bought BASIC), and (2) The amount of royalties we have received from sales to hobbyists makes the time spent on Altair BASIC worth less than $2 an hour.

Why is this? As the majority of hobbyists must be aware, most of you steal your software. Hardware must be paid for, but software is something to share. Who cares if the people who worked on it get paid?

Is this fair? One thing you don't do by stealing software is get back at MITS for some problem you may have had. MITS doesn't make money selling software. The royalty paid to us, the manual, the tape and the overhead make it a break-even operation. One thing you do do is prevent good software from being written. Who can afford to do professional work for nothing? What hobbyist can put 3-man years into programming, finding all bugs, documenting his product and distribute for free? The fact is, no one besides us has invested a lot of money in hobby software. We have written 6800 BASIC, and are writing 8080 APL and 6800 APL, but there is very little incentive to make this software available to hobbyists. Most directly, the thing you do is theft.

—Bill Gates, February 3, 1976

---

complain about appropriation of their content; the music industry worries about Napster-like Web sites that distribute music without license agreements. Napster was successfully sued in 2000 for violation of copyright, thus setting a standard for how all such Web sites will be treated by law in the future. Companies continue to push for new regulations that would better define, prevent, and penalize intellectual property violations in the vast world of cyberspace economics.

How should new legislation be shaped? The Uniform Computer Information Transactions Act (UCITA) is an attempt at defining uniform legal principles that would govern software and e-business transactions. As of 2001, Virginia and Maryland have adopted the legislation, but it has met with opposition from organizations like AFFECT (Americans For Fair Electronic Commerce Transactions), which argue that the legislation threatens privacy and consumer rights because it would allow companies to disable

A young Bill Gates created a storm of controversy among computer hobbyists with this 1976 open letter. Many computer users considered software to be something that should be shared freely; Gates took a very different view.

Estimated U.S. Trade Losses Due to Copyright Piracy 2000 and 2001
(in million dollars)

Total estimated losses								
	2001	2000		2001	2000		2001	2000
The Americas			Malaysia	328.5	140.0	Latvia	6.1	5.5
Argentina	189.2	350.8	Pakistan	124.2	144.5	Lithuania	12.4	12.0
Bolivia	27.4	26.8	Philippines	115.8	133.2	Moldova	5.0	6.0
Brazil	708.3	950.3	South Korea	652.1	400.2	Poland	261.4	248.8
Chile	61.6	82.1	Taiwan	332.9	553.7	Romania	37.7	43.0
Colombia	137.8	177.2	Thailand	130.3	245.8	Russian Federation	847.2	637.0
Costa Rica	13.7	20.1	Vietnam	26.3	28.5	Tajikistan	3.0	3.0
Dominican Republic	14.7	17.7	**Europe and C.I.S.**			Turkmenistan	0.0	5.0
Ecuador	27.2	8.2	Armenia	4.5	5.0	Ukraine	256.7	253.7
El Salvador	15.4	17.7	Azerbaijan	13.0	12.0	Uzbekistan	0.0	30.0
Guatemala	18.6	20.7	Belarus	20.0	28.0	**Middle East and Africa**		
Mexico	806.2	525.7	Bulgaria	19.8	16.6	Egypt	70.7	81.9
Paraguay	262.1	223.2	Czech Republic	101.9	97.1	Israel	159.4	164.3
Peru	82.0	84.9	Estonia	13.8	14.7	Kuwait	16.0	20.1
Uruguay	14.4	32.2	Georgia	6.0	5.0	Lebanon	13.1	14.8
Venezuela	124.7	140.9	Greece	48.9	112.0	Qatar	2.9	3.7
Asia/Pacific			Hungary	91.1	67.9	Saudi Arabia	188.1	107.7
China	1932.5	1085.1	Italy	542.3	540.5	South Africa	89.8	110.6
India	363.0	270.6	Kazakhstan	25.0	25.0	Turkey	126.6	276.8
Indonesia	88.5	134.3	Kyrgyzstan	8.0	10.0	**Total**	**9,639.2**	**8,744.3**

Source: International Intellectual Property Alliance, USTR 2002, "Special 301 Decisions and IIPA Estimated U.S. Trade Losses due to Copyright Piracy," July 2002.

The International Intellectual Property Alliance is a consortium of content producers; the Alliance has estimated the amount U.S. companies lost because of copyright piracy in 2000 and 2001 to be close to $10 billion.

software without notification, retroactively change the terms of the license, and permit licenses to which buyers do not have access until after purchase of the product (often referred to as "shrink-wrap" or "click-on" licenses). Groups like the Free Software Foundation maintain that UCITA favors big software companies and limits the rights and options of smaller ones.

Software companies like Microsoft have also come under attack for license restrictions that require customer use of Microsoft products. Industry watchdogs press for license laws that prevent such monopolistic practices.

Overarching all of these concerns is the fear that a proliferation of strict license agreements may impede technological progress. Critics argue that if software and e-business

get too bogged down in endless licensing disputes, the pace of innovation will slow. Thus, any new license laws must weigh the government's obligation to protect companies' rights against its obligation to encourage economic growth and innovation.

Further Reading

Gikkas, Nicholas S. "International Licensing of Intellectual Property: The Promise and the Peril." *Journal of Technology Law and Policy*, no. 1 (Spring 1996).
Also available: http://journal.law.ufl.edu/~techlaw/1/gikkas.html (February 19, 2003).
Kunze, Carol A. UCITA Online. http://www.ucitaonline.com (February 6, 2003).
Lessig, Lawrence. *The Future of Ideas: The Fate of the Commons in a Connected World.* New York: Random House, 2001.

—*Andrea Troyer and John Troyer*

Lowell Mills

In the nineteenth century, the city of Lowell, Massachusetts, was home to a thriving cotton textile industry. Lowell Mills was one of the earliest sites of the Industrial Revolution in the United States. Today the textile industry is gone, but the factories, machinery, canal system, and workers' boardinghouses from the Lowell Mills are preserved as the Lowell National Historic Park.

The Boston Manufacturing Company

Lowell was named after Francis Cabot Lowell, who established the first successful integrated textile factory in the United States, at Waltham, Massachusetts, on the Charles River. Lowell's mill was integrated because spinning and weaving were done under one roof. Spinning mills had previously been established in New England, but Lowell's mill was the first in the United States to employ mechanical looms for weaving.

Lowell, a wealthy Boston merchant, had visited England from 1810 to 1812 and smuggled out drawings of textile machinery used in the factories of Manchester. When he returned to Massachusetts, he and several friends formed the Boston Associates to raise capital and incorporated the Boston Manufacturing Company in 1813. This company was the first industrial corporation in the United States to be based upon the principle of limited liability (if the corporation fails, owners lose only the money they have invested and cannot be held liable for debts of the corporation). This corporate form of ownership allowed the Boston Associates to finance the first Waltham mill, which began operating in 1815, and later three additional mills in Waltham.

Using Lowell's sketches, skilled mechanic Paul Moody designed a factory that integrated a set of manufacturing steps from

See also:
Immigration; Industrial Revolution; Women in the Workforce.

A bird's-eye view of the mills in Lowell, Massachusetts, circa 1900.

The early mill-girls were of different ages. Some were not over ten years old; a few were in middle life, but the majority were between the ages of sixteen and twenty-five. The very young girls were called "doffers." They "doffed," or took off, the full bobbins from the spinning-frames, and replaced them with empty ones. These mites worked about fifteen minutes every hour and the rest of the time was their own. When the overseer was kind they were allowed to read, knit, or go outside the mill-yard to play. They were paid two dollars a week. The working hours of all the girls extended from five o'clock in the morning until seven in the evening, with one half-hour each, for breakfast and dinner. Even the doffers were forced to be on duty nearly fourteen hours a day. This was the greatest hardship in the lives of these children. Several years later a ten-hour law was passed, but not until long after some of these little doffers were old enough to appear before the legislative committee on the subject, and plead, by their presence, for a reduction of the hours of labor.

Source: Harriet H. Robertson, "Early Factory Labor in New England," in *Massachusetts Bureau of Statistics of Labor,* Fourteenth Annual Report, Boston, Wright & Potter, 1883.

In 1883 Harriet H. Robinson recalled some details of daily life in the mills for the very young girls who worked there.

processing raw cotton to finishing the cloth. Moody's designs adapted British technology to American conditions. By automating many processes that were still done by hand in England, Moody accelerated production and economized on skilled labor, which was much scarcer in the United States than in England.

The Establishment of Lowell

The cotton textile industry grew rapidly in New England, a region with many rivers

A 14-year-old girl working as a spool tender in a Lowell cotton mill, 1916.

and waterfalls that could be used to power waterwheels. After having built four mills in Waltham, the Boston Associates decided that they could not expand their operations sufficiently on the Charles River. In 1822 they began construction of a new factory on the Merrimack River, northwest of Boston. They purchased the assets of a private canal company and erected a large dam that powered not only their new cotton textile mill but other factories as well. The canal system grew steadily. By the middle of the nineteenth century, it comprised six miles of canals in Lowell, powering 10 major factory complexes owned by a number of firms. Although cotton textiles were the leading product of Lowell, woolen cloth, carpeting, and hosiery were also produced.

The Boston Associates brought to Lowell the labor system that Francis Lowell (who died in 1817) had established in Waltham. Finding male workers for the mills was difficult as most men preferred to work on their family farms or move west. Lowell, therefore, recruited farm girls, who had fewer opportunities for outside employment. To reassure anxious parents, Lowell built boardinghouses for the young women and provided strict supervision by boardinghouse matrons. The young women were required to attend church and observe a 10:00 P.M. curfew. They worked 12 or 13 hours a day, six days per week. Their lives were hard by today's standards, but probably no harder than their lives had been on the farm. Life at Lowell provided, moreover, certain advantages over rural life, including access to a wider circle of friends, new opportunities to meet young men, and the use of a circulating library and the chance to attend night-school classes. Most of the women worked at the mills only for a year or two, leaving when they married.

Labor unrest came to Lowell in the 1830s as mill owners, facing increasing competition, began to decrease the wages they paid and to increase the number of operations workers were required to perform. In protest, the mill workers participated in several "turnouts" (walkouts), but they failed to

Two boys employed by the Merrimac Mill in Lowell, Massachusetts, photographed by Lewis Hine in 1911.

stop the deterioration in working conditions. In the 1840s Lowell attracted a new wave of immigrants: Irish families fleeing the potato famine of the 1840s settled in the area, followed by French Canadians, Greeks, Poles, Portuguese, and others. The new immigrants, often willing to work for low wages, increasingly replaced New England women in the mills.

Lowell's textile industry brought into being and supported a flourishing machinery industry. Paul Moody headed the machine shop that supplied the machinery

---

The Song of the Spinners

The day is o'er, nor longer we toil and spin
For evening's hush withdraws from the
* daily din*
And now we sing, with gladsome hearts,
The theme of the spinner's song
That labor to leisure a zest imparts
Unknown to the idle throng.

We spin all day, and then in time for rest,
Sweet peace is found, a joyous welcome
* guest.*
Despite of toil we all agree,
Or out of the Mills or in,
Dependent on others we ne'er will be
So long as we're able to spin.

Source: Lowell Offering, 1841.

For many young women, work at the Lowell Mills presented them with a level of opportunity they could not get elsewhere.

Restored looms at the Boott Cotton Mills Museum, part of Lowell Mills National Historic Park.

for the Waltham mills, and he moved to Lowell with the Boston Associates. In 1835 his machine shop began producing locomotives; later it produced hydraulic turbines, which replaced waterwheels as the major power source for factories in Lowell and elsewhere.

Lowell's textile mills continued to prosper through 1860. Advances in technology greatly lowered the costs of producing cloth, thus enabling suppliers to lower the prices they charged consumers. At the same time, the nation's population was growing and incomes were increasing, adding to consumer demand. By 1860 the cotton textile industry was the largest manufacturing industry in the United States.

During the last decades of the nineteenth century, the textile industry began to shift to the southern states, where labor costs were lower, and the Lowell mills began to close. The last major mills were shut in the 1950s.

In 1978 the Lowell National Historic Park opened, with mills, canals, and boardinghouses restored and maintained by the U.S. National Park Service. Visitors to the park may now walk among the mill floors and related facilities where young women and immigrant workers once sustained perhaps the most important enterprise of the U.S. Industrial Revolution.

Further Reading

Dalzell, Robert F. *Enterprising Elite: The Boston Associates and the World They Made.* Cambridge, Mass.: Harvard University Press, 1987.

Dublin, Thomas. *Lowell: The Story of an Industrial City.* Washington, D.C.: U.S. Department of the Interior, National Park Service, 1992.

Weisman, JoAnne B., ed. *The Lowell Mill Girls: Life in the Factory.* Lowell, Mass.: Discover Enterprises, 1991.

—*Jean Caldwell*

Macroeconomics

Traditionally economics has been divided into two areas: microeconomics and macroeconomics. The two terms are derived from Greek: *micro,* meaning small, and *macro,* meaning large. Microeconomics is the study of individual consumers, workers, and producers functioning in specific markets. It explores how those individuals and markets function and generate (or do not generate) efficient outcomes for a society. Macroeconomics uses many of the same tools, but focuses on somewhat different problems. While microeconomics focuses on individuals, firms, and specific markets, macroeconomics considers the behavior of the economy as a whole—all individuals, firms, and markets together.

For example, the determination of stock and bond prices and the functioning of individual banks fall under the purview of microeconomics, while the effects of

See also:
Business Cycles; Economic Growth; Fiscal Policy; Inflation; Microeconomics; Monetary Policy.

Macroeconomics founder John Maynard Keynes in his study in 1940.

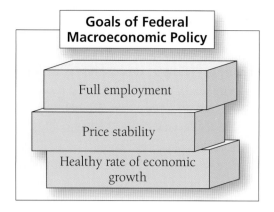

Goals of Federal Macroeconomic Policy

Full employment

Price stability

Healthy rate of economic growth

changes in stock prices on investors' overall spending plans and the effects of changes in interest rates on total spending are macroeconomic issues. The trend in economic research and understanding has been increasingly to apply the principles of microeconomics to many of the issues studied in macroeconomics.

In 1936 John Maynard Keynes published his *General Theory of Employment, Interest, and Money*, which began the study of macroeconomics. At the time, the United States and much of the rest of the developed world were in the midst of the Great Depression, with unemployment rates above 25 percent and economic activity shrinking significantly. Keynes analyzed how consumption and investment spending are determined and how fluctuations in spending can cause unemployment and falling output.

Macroeconomics begins with the generation of data that describe conditions in the economy. For example, levels of employment and unemployment and the percentage of the labor force that is unemployed make up one set of indicators of conditions in a country's economy. Index numbers are used to measure average price

levels; changes in those index numbers give us rates of inflation—the rise in the average or overall level of prices. A number of different indexes are used, depending upon the goods and services included in the index. The most well known is the Consumer Price Index, which calculates average price levels for a collection of goods and services (called a market basket) that a typical consumer might buy. Another measure of economic well-being is an estimate of total production in the entire economy during a year, the real gross domestic product (GDP). These measures indicate the status of unemployment, inflation, and growth, and help us understand how well the economy is doing in relation to its potential.

Perhaps the most important area of study within macroeconomics is economic growth. Growth in real GDP per person raises standards of living and explains differences in incomes among individuals in different countries. Considerable effort has been and continues to be devoted to identifying the importance of technological advances, the amount and skills of labor, and the quantity and kind of investment spending in determining the rate of growth in an economy over time.

Macroeconomics includes analysis of the determinants of spending in relation to an economy's capacity. GDP consists of a number of different kinds of spending: consumption, investment, government, and net export spending. Fluctuations in any of these kinds of spending cause total spending to change and can cause temporary periods of inflation or unemployment. Research has helped economists and politicians understand that a trade-off between

Tools of Government Economic Policy

Fiscal Policy
The use of spending and taxing powers to influence total spending, investing, and saving.

Monetary Policy
The ability of the Federal Reserve System to manage the amount of money circulating in the economy.

Three Primary Macroeconomic Indicators

Indicator	Function	Key Index
• Unemployment rate	• Measures underutilization of labor in nation	• Unemployment rate
• Inflation rate	• Measures rate of change in average level of prices	• Consumer Price Index
• Growth rate in real national output	• Measures pace of what economy is producing in goods and services	• Gross domestic product

unemployment and inflation is sometimes necessary. At other times, they both can move in the same direction.

Macroeconomics and Politics

Government policies about how and whether to respond to periods of rising unemployment, rising inflation, or falling real GDP are important, often controversial, parts of macroeconomics, which affects both fiscal and monetary policy. Fiscal policy is the federal government's use of its spending and taxing powers to influence total spending, investing, and saving in the economy and thereby encourage economic growth, reduce inflationary pressures, or decrease unemployment. The effectiveness of those policies and how best to manage fiscal policy are important matters of research and debate. The roles of government deficits and surpluses, as well as changes in government debt, are also important macroeconomic issues.

Monetary policy is the ability of the Federal Reserve System to manage the amount of money that circulates in the economy. Changes in the money supply and in interest rates influence businesses in making decisions about spending on new plants and machinery, and individuals in purchasing automobiles, appliances, and homes. Changes in the money supply help determine total spending. Because of the importance of the availability of money and the level of interest rates, a field known as money and banking is included in macroeconomics. The study of the banking system, how loans are made, and even how money is created are key components of the field.

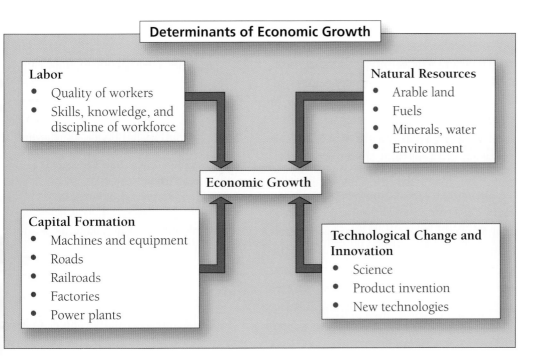

Determinants of Economic Growth

Labor
- Quality of workers
- Skills, knowledge, and discipline of workforce

Natural Resources
- Arable land
- Fuels
- Minerals, water
- Environment

Economic Growth

Capital Formation
- Machines and equipment
- Roads
- Railroads
- Factories
- Power plants

Technological Change and Innovation
- Science
- Product invention
- New technologies

Schools of Macroeconomics

School	Themes
• Classical	• Advocates laissez-faire. Government should allow the economy to function without interference.
• Keynesian	• Stresses primacy of fiscal policy in influencing output and employment. In times of depression the government should run deficits; in times of inflation it should have surpluses.
• Monetarist	• Emphasizes the importance of monetary policy to influence macroeconomic activity over the short term. Advocates fixed rate of growth of money supply through all economic conditions.
• New classical economist	• Predictable macroeconomic policies have no real effect on output or employment because people anticipate government actions and act to protect their interests, thereby negating government policy.

Macroeconomics is not without its controversies, particularly on the frontier of research and new understanding of how our overall economy works and how best to use policy. Although Keynes proposed using fiscal policy to bring the world out of the Depression, he also argued that monetary policy is ineffective in stimulating spending. Later, other researchers, led by Milton Friedman, provided evidence that not only is monetary policy effective, it is so effective that mistakes are often made. They found that mistakes in monetary policy are the cause of most periods of inflation, and they argued that fiscal policy is difficult to use and often ineffective.

Controversy exists over the implementation of macroeconomic policy. Because policies take time to influence output, employment, and inflation, effective use of policy requires the forecasting of future conditions and acting in the present to influence the future. However, forecasts tend to be imprecise, which leads to mistakes that may actually worsen conditions.

Macroeconomic issues and concerns are on the front pages of newspapers almost daily. The unemployment, inflation, and economic growth announcements receive significant attention as indicators of how well the economy is working. Political parties often debate spending and taxing policies that may improve conditions. The Federal Reserve policy committee meets approximately every six weeks to discuss economic conditions and whether monetary policy should be changed. Understanding how the overall economy works and how policy functions are important tools in developing an understanding of modern societies.

Further Reading

Agénor, Pierre-Richard, and Peter J. Montiel. *Development Macroeconomics*. 2nd ed. Princeton, N.J. : Princeton University Press, 1999.

Blanchard, Olivier. *Macroeconomics*. 2nd ed. Upper Saddle River, N.J.: Prentice-Hall, 2000.

Breit, William, and Roger L. Ransom. *The Academic Scribblers*. 3rd ed. Princeton, N.J.: Princeton University Press, 1998.

Carson, Robert Barry, Wade L. Thomas, and Jason Hecht. *Macroeconomic Issues Today: Alternative Approaches*. 6th ed. Armonk, N.Y.: M. E. Sharpe, 1999.

Gaske, Daniel. *Understanding U.S. and Global Economic Trends: A Guide for the Non-Economist*. 2nd ed. Dubuque, Iowa: Kendall/Hunt, 1999.

Heilbroner, Robert L. *The Worldly Philosophers: The Lives, Times, and Ideas of the Great Economic Thinkers*. Rev. 7th ed. New York: Simon & Schuster, 1999.

Kennedy, Peter. *Macroeconomic Essentials: Understanding Economics in the News*. 2nd ed. Cambridge, Mass.: MIT Press, 2000.

Keynes, John Maynard. *The General Theory of Employment, Interest and Money*. New York: Harcourt, Brace, 1936.

Mankiw, N. Gregory. *Principles of Macroeconomics*. 2nd ed. Cincinnati, Ohio: South-Western Publishing, 2000.

—*Stephen Buckles*

Major League Baseball Players Association

Founded in 1965, the Major League Baseball Players Association (MLBPA) rose to become the nation's most powerful union. It won free agency for players in 1976, ushering in an era of rapidly rising salaries in baseball and other sports. Professional athletes are not members of the struggling working class celebrated in folk songs. Even so, baseball's 1,200-member union forged a solidarity among players that created a significant success story for organized labor.

Working conditions for baseball players in the pre-union era were fairly difficult: The pay was quite low (many players had second jobs); careers were short; and in the early days, pension programs were extremely rare, as were opportunities to "cash in" on celebrity through media endorsements. Throughout the history of the sport, players had tried to organize, starting with the Brotherhood of Professional Baseball Players in 1885. Other attempts came in 1900, 1912, and 1946. Each time, weak organizations crumbled after a few years without winning concessions from owners.

The players finally had some success when they hired Marvin Miller, an economist with the United Steelworkers of America, as the new union's first executive director in 1966. Once in office, Miller launched what amounted to an education campaign among players, convincing a skeptical membership that owners were taking advantage of players and that sticking together was the way to redress grievances. In 1968 the Players Association negotiated the first collective bargaining agreement in professional sports. However, the union's greatest achievement came in the next decade with the dismantling of the "reserve clause."

An artifact of the 1880s that was part of the standard player contract, the reserve clause tied a player to one team for his entire career. In 1969 St. Louis Cardinals outfielder Curt Flood objected to a trade to the Philadelphia Phillies. He filed a lawsuit against major league baseball to challenge the reserve clause as a violation of federal antitrust laws. Flood lost his suit in 1972, but the battle against the reserve clause had been joined.

Three years later, independent arbitrator Peter Seitz brought an end to the system by ruling that the reserve clause gave teams exclusive rights to a player only for one year, not his entire career. The immediate effect of the ruling was to make free agents of pitchers Andy Messersmith and Dave McNally; the long-term effects changed baseball.

When teams competed for star players, salaries increased, not just for the big names but for the journeymen as well. The average ballplayer earned $51,501 in 1976, or 1.5 times the nation's average household income. In 2001 baseball's average salary rose to $2.1

See also:
Collective Bargaining;
Compensation; Labor Union;
Sports Industry.

Curt Flood of the St. Louis Cardinals in 1967.

million, 50 times the national average. Free agency spread to other sports, and as professional sports as a whole evolved into a multibillion-dollar industry, players were free to negotiate for their piece of the pie. By 2001 the average salary had soared to $4.2 million in basketball, $1.2 million in football, and $1.4 million in hockey.

Free agency was not the MLBPA's only achievement. It has also negotiated for higher minimum salaries, salary arbitration, bigger pensions, and broader licensing rights.

None of these victories came easily. The rise of the players' unions brought labor strife to baseball and other sports. Baseball has a long history of acrimonious relations between owners and players, with work stoppages marking the expiration of nearly every collective bargaining agreement.

In 1985 fans at Yankee Stadium express their feelings about a possible baseball strike.

Baseball's first strike took place in 1972, lasting two weeks and wiping out 86 games. Seven more strikes and lockouts occurred over the next two decades, including a 50-day strike in 1981 that cost the sport 712 games. The most disruptive strike lasted 232 days, eliminating 938 games at the end of 1994 and the start of 1995, and leading to cancellation of the World Series for the first time since 1904. The protracted labor dispute disillusioned many fans, and five years were needed for attendance to return to prestrike levels.

As their unions came of age, other sports have also encountered labor troubles. In football and basketball, the battle between labor and management led to salary caps that imposed some restraint on player pay. Faced with the most powerful

Major League Baseball Players Association

1885
Brotherhood of Professional Baseball Players is the first attempt at a baseball union.

1965
Major League Baseball Players Association (MLBA) is founded.

1968
MLBA negotiates the first collective bargaining agreement in professional sports.

1969
Cardinals' outfielder Curt Flood files anti-trust lawsuit against Major League Baseball.

1972
Baseball's first strike takes place.

1976
MLBA wins free agency for its players.

2001
Baseball's average salary rises to $2.1 million, 50 times the national average.

Jason Giambi (left) shakes hands with Yankees' general manager Brian Cahsman in 2001. The Yankees signed Giambi to a seven-year contract for $120 million.

union in professional sports, baseball's owners have not succeeded in imposing a salary cap.

Baseball's most recent collective bargaining agreement expired at the end of the 2001 season. Remembering the fans' reaction to the 1994–1995 strike, neither side wanted another work stoppage. Negotiations on a new collective bargaining agreement concluded successfully in 2002 with an extraordinary agreement, featuring revenue sharing and a luxury tax, in which teams whose player salaries cross a set threshold will have to pay a tax that will be used to shore up the poorer teams.

Further Reading

Abrams, Roger I. *Legal Bases: Baseball and the Law*. Philadelphia: Temple University Press, 1998.

Helyar, John. *Lords of the Realm: The Real History of Baseball*. New York: Villard Books, 1994.

Miller, Marvin. *A Whole Different Ball Game: The Sport and Business of Baseball*. New York: Birch Lane Press, 1991.

—*Richard Alm*

See also:
Capitalism;
Environmentalism; Smith,
Adam; Sustainable
Development.

Malthus, Thomas Robert

1766–1834
Economist

Thomas Robert Malthus made an important contribution to the development of economic thought with *An Essay on the Principle of Population,* which he published anonymously in 1798 and revised and reissued in a second edition in 1803. The work created an instant controversy because of its departure from the progressive optimism of the eighteenth-century Enlightenment and from the liberal school of economic thought founded by Adam Smith. Malthus's ideas have continued to fuel debates in development economics, in environmental science, and in the philosophy of distributive justice.

Malthus was born in Guildford in Surrey, England. He was educated at Jesus College, Cambridge, before joining the Church of England in 1788 and serving briefly as curate of a Surrey parish. In 1805 he was appointed professor of history and political economy at Haileybury College, a post he occupied for the remainder of his life.

Malthus was the first thinker to designate population growth as an economic problem. Smith had argued that the free market would ensure against the risk of over- or underpopulation. He suggested that the demand for labor would increase as the economy grew, which, in turn, would increase workers' wages, making them able to support larger families. Wages would then decline to reflect this change in the supply of labor, thereby decreasing rates of reproduction.

However, the predominant view of population came not from the theoretical deductions of Smith but from the demographic observations of the Anglican clergyman William Paley. Contrary to Smith, Paley argued that a growing workforce was the source of economic development and of national strength. Working from the crude data available in the eighteenth century, Paley warned that the British population was declining, with potentially catastrophic consequences for the economy and for the security of the realm.

Using figures on rapid population growth compiled by Benjamin Franklin in the United States, Malthus reached the opposite conclusion: an increase in population threatened disaster. Malthus wrote that two fundamental human needs—for food and for reproduction—were in conflict. According to Malthus, unchecked population growth proceeded geometrically (that is, multiplied by a constant, for example, 2,

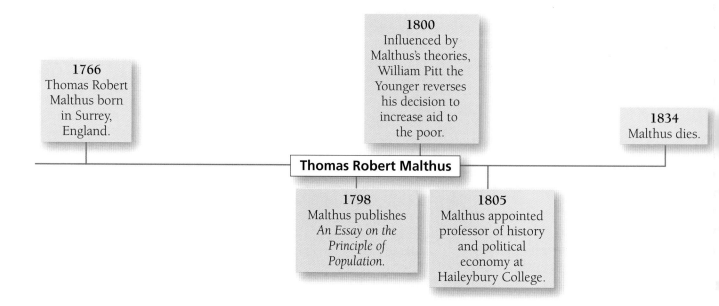

1766
Thomas Robert Malthus born in Surrey, England.

1800
Influenced by Malthus's theories, William Pitt the Younger reverses his decision to increase aid to the poor.

1834
Malthus dies.

Thomas Robert Malthus

1798
Malthus publishes *An Essay on the Principle of Population.*

1805
Malthus appointed professor of history and political economy at Haileybury College.

4, 8, 16, 32, 64), whereas the growth in the food supply was arithmetical (added by a constant, for example, 1, 2, 3, 4, 5). The inevitable result was that the number of units of food available on a per capita basis must fall over time.

In contrast to Smith, Malthus argued that population could be self-regulating only at the cost of social misery. He used the term "positive checks" to describe phenomena such as war, plague, and famine, which regulated population through increasing the death rate. More desirable were "preventive checks" that reduced the birth rate through self-restraint and sexual abstinence. In the social context of the time, contraception and abortion were primitive, hazardous, and subject to severe social and legal prohibition. Realistically, Malthus claimed, preventive checks could be expected only of the educated upper classes.

Malthus's ideas had immediate political and intellectual impact. In 1796 prime minister William Pitt the Younger, influenced by Paley's ideas, had committed himself to an increase in the level of relief distributed to the poor as a means of boosting the population. In 1800, however, after exposure to the arguments of Malthus, Pitt reversed his decision, arguing that any increase in the numbers of the poor would lead to the application of the positive checks. Charles Darwin acknowledged Malthus's ideas about the competition for scarce resources as a major influence on the development of the evolutionary theory of natural selection. Furthermore, social Darwinist thinkers, including Herbert Spencer in his *Man versus the State* (1884), drew on Malthus to support their arguments against social welfare programs. The closing decades of the nineteenth century saw the rise of collectivist ideas asserting the benign potential of the state. Subsequently, Malthus's theories were marginalized, as comprehensive welfare states emerged over the course of the twentieth century.

The environmental movement of the 1960s revived interest in Malthus. In 1968

the American biologist Paul Ehrlich published his neo-Malthusian *The Population Bomb*, in which he warned that the rate of human reproduction would lead to an environmental catastrophe. This outcome could be avoided only by urgent measures to slow, or even reverse, population growth, including the spread of contraception and changes in government policies on taxes, benefits, and overseas aid in order to penalize large families and reward small ones.

Ehrlich's supporters found evidence for his case in the African famines of the 1970s

An undated engraving of Thomas Robert Malthus.

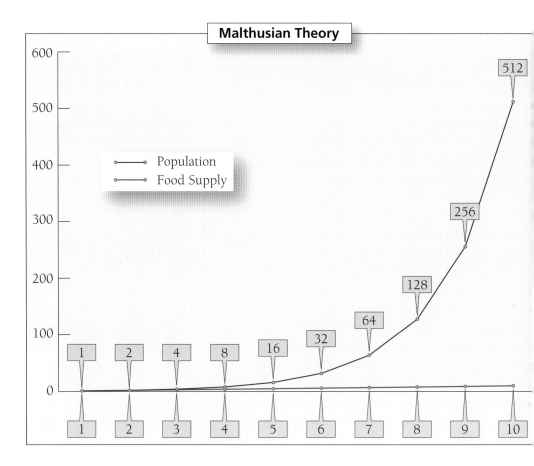

Malthusian Theory

Malthusian theory: population increases geometrically while resources increase arithmetically.

and 1980s. Malthusian ideas also underlay the decision of Indian prime minister Indira Gandhi to introduce a government program of forced sterilization during her country's economic crisis (1975–1977). The urgency of the environmental debate was heightened in 1972, when the Club of Rome, a nongovernmental think tank, produced its influential report *Limits to Growth*, which argued that population growth, in combination with industrial expansion, was rapidly exhausting the planet's finite supply of natural resources.

In the late twentieth century, however, Malthus's arguments were undermined by four factors. First, the rate of growth in agricultural productivity has been far greater than Malthus predicted. Second, economists like Amartya Sen have shown that famines tend to result not from economic or technical causes but from political conditions of dictatorship or war. Third, as natural resources have become scarcer, their market price has increased, leading to more efficient consumption or to the development of alternatives. Fourth, economic development reduces birth rates in advanced industria countries because wealthier and better-educated families have fewer children; the technology of birth control becomes more effective and socially more acceptable; and women secure greater reproductive right: and more autonomy. Nonetheless, Malthu: remains a central economic thinker whose writings mark the origin of the science o demography.

Further Reading

Brown, Lester Russell, Gary Gardner, and Brian Halweil. *Beyond Malthus: Nineteen Dimensions of the Population Challenge.* New York: W. W. Norton, 1999.

Ehrlich, Paul. *The Population Bomb.* 1968. Reprint, Cutchogue, N.Y.: Bucaneer Books, 1997.

Hollander, Samuel. *The Economics of Thomas Robert Malthus.* Toronto: University of Toronto Press, 1997.

Malthus, Thomas Robert. *An Essay on the Principle o Population.* 1798. Reprint, London: Penguin, 1985.

Petersen, William. *Malthus.* New Brunswick, N.J.: Transaction Publishers, 1999.

—*Peter C. Grosveno*

Management

Management is work done by supervisory individuals (managers) responsible for guiding formal organizations toward accomplishing their intended purposes. Management includes providing vision and leadership, establishing environments for effective work, analyzing and solving problems, making decisions, fostering communication, and ensuring accountability.

Modern concepts of management have evolved together with the large organizations that arose during and after the Industrial Revolution. Management is now a popular field of study in colleges and universities at both the undergraduate and graduate levels, and many people use the study of management to prepare themselves for eventual assignment to managerial responsibilities. Formal study is not an absolute requirement for becoming a manager—many managers have learned management on the job.

Managerial Functions

Just as there is no one way to manage, there is no comprehensive, precisely defined theory of management. Over the years, however, managers and people who study management have developed a substantial body of knowledge. Most management textbooks published since about 1950 have emphasized a functional approach based on the writings of management theory pioneers like Henri Fayol (1841–1925). Of the managerial functions Fayol identified, the ones most commonly referred to are planning, organizing, directing, and controlling.

Planning is a decision-making process in which managers set goals and objectives (consistent with their organizational purpose), select courses of action, make action assignments, determine means of assessment, allocate resources (typically through budgets), and authorize actions to be taken. Plans can specify unique, one-time sets of actions to be undertaken for special purposes, for example, designing a new model of a car, or routine, recurring sets of actions directed to recurring requirements, for example, managing university students' registration for courses. Decisions made within the plan may rely on conceptual analysis and judgment as well as a variety of quantitative analytic methods. Computers and database systems are vital aids to today's managers in planning and making decisions.

Organizing is the process managers use to structure organizations, design jobs, and select and assign people to individual jobs and work groups. Two critical aspects of organizing are authority (the legal right to direct certain actions) and responsibility (a moral requirement to do certain things and behave in certain ways). Authority, responsibility, and channels of communication are necessary for empowering and coordinating the actions of an organization's members. Managers delegate authority (empower others to act) and determine the means of communication to be used in the activity in question.

Managers, however, never surrender responsibility. A manager who empowers a subordinate to take certain actions or perform specific tasks is considered to be responsible for the outcome even if the subordinate fails to perform. Delegation is important because, especially in large organizations, managers must rely on others to shoulder part of the workload. As organizations grow, the need for increased delegation fosters the creation of additional levels of managerial responsibility, often clustered according to organizational functions like production, marketing, and

See also:
Business Ethics; Human Resources; Management Theory; Total Quality Management.

Henri Fayol's basic management principles.

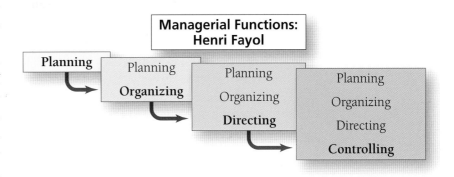

Good management often involves leading and inspiring workers rather than simply asserting authority over them.

finance. The model for complex, formal organizations was described by the German sociologist Max Weber (1864–1920).

Directing is the process managers use to mobilize, engage, and guide the actions of members of the organization. Directing depends upon four essential components: power (the ability to compel compliance), leadership (inspiring and guiding), motivation (arousing the ability and desire to be productive), and communication (effectively exchanging meaning). Many modern textbooks speak of leading rather than directing in describing this managerial function.

Managers possess several kinds of power. Depending upon the circumstances hey can give orders, reward performance, punish failure or improper behavior, and employ expertise and social skills to guide and encourage their subordinates. Power alone is usually not sufficient for managers to be successful in supervising others.

Communication is the process of exchanging meaning between two or more individuals. Managers must become skilled at receiving and interpreting messages, at creating and transmitting messages, and at providing or seeking feedback. Managers must therefore write well and speak effectively to a wide variety of audiences, but that is not sufficient. Managers must also learn to solicit information, invite the input of others, share information effectively, be able to shape information from raw data, and master modern communication technologies. The directing function is rendered impotent without effective communication.

Controlling is how managers evaluate the effectiveness of plans and decisions made. It requires setting standards for performance, measuring performance against standards, determining whether significant deviations exist, and, if they do, making corrections as necessary to revise the plan of action, adjust performance standards, or correct performance failures. Controlling is the partner of planning. Just as planning is useless without a means to evaluate effectiveness, controlling in the absence of planning is equally inappropriate.

Managerial Functions Applied

The managerial functions described above provide a general, abstract picture of management. Managers do not work in the abstract, however; they manage real people and projects, and they are responsible for the effectiveness and efficiency of actual organizations. In planning, organizing, directing, and controlling, they apply themselves to a range of business activities including:

- *Marketing*—defining the customer and the customer's needs, selecting products and services, designing advertising

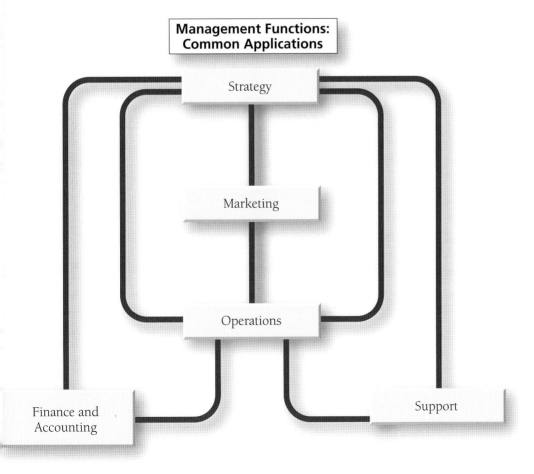

Finance and accounting, and support functions like office and facilities management, form a foundation for the more product- and sales-oriented management functions including operations, marketing, and strategy.

Leadership and Motivation

Leadership is a much used but much misunderstood term. Leadership and management are not synonymous, although many people use the term *leadership* when referring to organizational managers as organizational leaders. Leadership is the ability to gain the willing compliance of others in doing what the leader wants done. Leadership ability is closely related to the personality of the leader, but being an effective leader is not the result of following a set of given procedures. Obviously, developing leadership skills is very useful to a manager. Power can force others to comply, but leadership can inspire others to go beyond mere compliance.

Motivation is the force that drives individuals to act and sustains them in their action. In general, job performance depends upon a worker's ability (mental and physical capacity), skill (ability refined and improved through practice, learning, and experience), and motivation (the desire to perform to a certain level). Although ability and skill are obviously important, low levels of motivation can adversely affect able, skilled workers, decreasing their productivity. Managers, therefore, must strive to increase workers' motivation.

Unfortunately, as is the case with leadership, no simple, fail-safe procedure is available to address motivational shortfalls. Some theories emphasize human needs (what motivates people?), some focus on the process of motivation (how does motivation occur and how do individuals choose to be motivated?), and some emphasize behavior reinforcement. Probably most important for managers to understand is that a worker's motivation is "owned by" the worker, not by the manager, and must be addressed by leadership skills, not merely authority.

and promotional material, determining prices, and providing products and services to customers in convenient ways or places.

- *Operations*—designing and operating the processes and systems by which firms create and make products and services available to marketers.
- *Finance and Accounting*—acquiring and managing financial resources including invested, borrowed, and operating cash.
- *Support*—managing necessary auxiliary actions, including human resources, physical plant, insurance, legal, security, and information processing.
- *Strategy*—supervising all organizational functions and functional managers simultaneously to ensure that all the pieces fit together.

In small, entrepreneurial businesses, the owners perform all of these actions. Because of the risks and challenges involved in juggling so many activities, the world of the entrepreneurial owner–manager looks especially exciting and attractive to some people and daunting to others.

Every generation of managers must contend with important social, political, legal, economic, and ecological realities specific to their era. Managers in the twenty-first century must pay attention to issues of equal opportunity and diversity, frequent litigation, a network of laws and regulations, differing perspectives rooted in the age and experience levels of employees and customers, electronic commerce and the Internet, global competition, economic cycles, rapid technological change, pollution control, worker safety and quality of work life, and recurring challenges to ethical and socially responsive behavior.

Individuals can learn about management by reviewing relevant scholarship and by observing managers in action. They should assess themselves, too, determining whether they want to be accountable for the behavior and performance of others in organizational settings. They should want to influence others for work-related betterment. They should develop skills in mastering the functions of management and managerial roles through actual managerial experience. Potential managers must be able to deal with complexity, handle multiple and often divergent demands, and not be dismayed by unpredictable human behavior. In a competitive business climate, managers must also grasp the relationship between product or service quality and business success.

Further Reading

Fayol, Henri. *General and Industrial Management.* 1949. Reprint, New York: Institute of Electrical and Electronics Engineers, 1984.

Hellriegel, Don, Susan E. Jackson, and John W. Slocum, Jr. *Management: A Competency-Based Approach.* 9th ed. Cincinnati, Ohio: South-Western, 2002.

Koontz, Harold, and Heinz Weihrich. *Management.* 10th ed. New York: McGraw-Hill, 1993.

Weber, Max. *Max Weber: The Theory of Social and Economic Organization.* Translated by A. M. Henderson and Talcott Parsons. New York: Free Press, 1964.

—*John Washbush*

Management Theory

One of the most dramatic changes in the United States over the course of the twentieth century was the transformation of work—the nation in which most people worked on farms or as individual artisans has changed to a nation in which most seek careers and employment in formal organizations. Formal organizations are social structures that are relatively stable, are formed to perform specific actions and produce specific outcomes, and have relative permanence. The people who run these organizations are called managers. Managers supervise, guide, and direct others; set organizational goals and objectives; make critical organizational decisions; and determine how the organization is going to remain in existence.

Does a body of systematic theory and learning about managers' functions exist? Unfortunately, not quite. Although management is taught in most postsecondary schools, no academic discipline (a coherent, unified body of knowledge) of management has yet been developed. At best, there are theories of management. Thus, management can be considered theoretical to the extent that a body of knowledge about it is available, but management is also represented by skill in application of that knowledge and by effectively learning from experience.

Classical Theory

To a considerable extent, modern organizations are products of the eighteenth and nineteenth centuries, which produced the Industrial Revolution, large nation-states, and urbanization. The resulting large organizations, now so common, required structure and direction. During the last quarter of the nineteenth century, a number of individuals began to write systematically about and discuss formal organizations and the people that were assigned to manage, or

administer, them. These discussions focused on technical issues related to how to design jobs and how to best integrate them to provide effectiveness (achieve intended outcomes) and efficiency (best use of available resources and avoidance of waste).

Typical of this structural focus are the writings of the German sociologist Max Weber, who described a rational, legal bureaucracy providing an organizational model built on positions, responsibilities, and authority of office. The writings of U.S. engineer and management consultant Frederick W. Taylor, known as the father of scientific management, discussed how best

See also:
Drucker, Peter; Management; Total Quality Management.

Frederick W. Taylor, author of The Principles of Scientific Management *(1911).*

to design individual jobs to generate high standards of productivity and levels of output. The French industrialist Henri Fayol defined management functions (the kinds of activities managers perform) and provided a list of principles for effective management. The emphasis in all these writings was on systematic and rational analysis of the "best" way to achieve specific objectives at organizational, job, and managerial levels.

From the perspective of management theory, probably the most important was Fayol. He also argued that management could and should be taught, thus giving it status as a profession and spawning a vast array of books, articles, and academic and training programs. Most modern textbooks on management use the concept of management functions as an essential framework. Fayol proposed that managerial work is characterized by the performance of the following functions:

- Planning (defining ends and the means to them)
- Organizing (structuring organizations and work groups, and designing jobs)

- Commanding (exercising authority and supervising and directing the actions of others)
- Coordinating (effectively interrelating jobs, managers and organizational components through communication)
- Controlling (determining outcomes, comparing performance to intentions and expectations, and taking appropriate corrective action if significant deviations are found)

Additionally, Fayol proposed a list of principles (basic, but nonrigid, guidelines for managerial performance). For much of the twentieth century, many books on management emphasized the concept of principles like unity of command, unity of direction, order, and discipline (see box).

To a considerable extent, the perspectives of the Classical School of management theorists provide the underpinnings of modern organizations. In particular, modern industrial organizations owe a considerable debt to the work of Taylor and his disciples Henry L. Gantt (father of the Gantt chart, which continues to be used for planning and controlling) and the

Principles of Management

Although principles like Henri Fayol's have often been criticized as simplistic and overbearing, most people with organizational experience would agree that such principles are reasonable general guidelines for managers and promote desirable organizational characteristics.

- Division of work (specialization)
- Authority and responsibility (authority in direct relation to responsibility)
- Discipline (respect, obedience, and energy)
- Unity of command (subordinates have only one supervisor)
- Unity of direction (a coherent, integrated set of plans)
- Subordination of individual to general interest
- Remuneration (fair pay that motivates and rewards)
- Centralization (balancing with decentralization)
- Scalar chair (hierarchical linkages)
- Order (proper organization of people and things)
- Equity (loyalty related to kindness and justice)
- Stability of tenure (avoiding excessive personnel turnover)
- Initiative (fostering creative, analytic thinking)

Project: Term Paper	Week												
	1	2	3	4	5	6	7	8	9	10	11	12	13
Tasks													
Determine viability of project	■	■											
Speak to adviser about project		■											
Prepare proposal			■										
Get formal acceptance of proposal				■	■								
Research project						■	■						
Write first draft							■	■	■				
Submit to adviser for preliminary review										■			
Revise draft											■	■	
Submit final paper													■

Gilbreths (Frank B. and Lillian M., who did pioneering work in job design and helped create concepts and methods of time and motion study). The modern fields of industrial engineering and production and operations management are direct descendants of these scholars.

Behavioral Theory

One of the failings of the Classical School was its relatively simplistic understanding of human behavior and the degree to which managers need to develop broad and comprehensive understandings of how individuals, groups, social realities, and work interact and affect job performance. For the most part, the Classicists believed that workers were primarily influenced by economic factors (wages in particular).

These shortcomings began to be highlighted in the 1920s and 1930s by the famous Hawthorne Studies, conducted at a Western Electric plant near Chicago (a manufacturing plant for telephone equipment used by Bell Telephone). In a series of studies, the researchers discovered that managerial attention, group dynamics, and communication could affect productivity in positive ways. These studies also identified two organizational structures present in any organizational situation—the formal organization, which defines jobs, relationships, groupings, supervision, and structures, and the informal organization, which describes how people in the organization interact for purely social purposes.

This awakening to the effect and potential of human behavior led to examinations of ways to align worker behavior with the need for organizational productivity and performance. On the positive side, these studies led to the realization that managers need to improve their understanding of people and groups in organizational situations. On the negative side, early studies were overly strong in their suggestions that human relations concepts like listening, trying to boost morale, and improving wages and working conditions would automatically lead to improved worker performance. With the passage of time and rigorous application of the emerging behavioral sciences (psychology, sociology, and anthropology), more sophisticated understandings of organizational behavior were developed in terms of job motivation, leadership, communication, behavioral implications of job design, training, participation, group dynamics, and team building. Some researchers and theorists went so far as to suggest that their behavioral insights were the most essential information for managers, but management theory takes a more balanced approach today.

Quantitative Analysis and Management Science

Beginning in the 1950s, management theorists and scholars in disciplines like mathematics,

A Gantt chart provides a schedule that helps to plan, coordinate, and track tasks. Managers often use Gantt charts to illustrate the timing and duration of the phases of a project.

statistics, and the emerging field of computer science discovered and developed quantitative analytic techniques (employing mathematical models and problem solving) that had general applicability to a wide range of organizational situations and problems. These included methods for analyzing costs, studying competitors, and forecasting demand.

The creation and rapid development of computer technology (both hardware and software) have been prime factors in such theoretical breakthroughs. For example, modern spreadsheet programs, readily available to personal computer users, are not based on new concepts. Accountants used spreadsheets for many years, but in tedious pencil-and-paper form. The computer enables the user not only to structure and array numbers but also to change them, evaluate the impact of changes (conducting "what-if" analyses), and perform sophisticated mathematical and statistical analyses on the arrayed numbers. Although few have argued that these methods and techniques could be considered the essence of management, the techniques and methods are so important and sufficiently useful that all managers should have acquaintance with them and develop the ability to use them.

Systems and Contingencies

As these three major threads of thought formed and developed, two additional threads began to influence management theory. The first was systems theory. A system is a set of interacting parts that together form a unified whole. Organizations are complex social–technical systems, and managers need to understand how the people and the parts interact and affect each other. Organizations are open systems—they exist in and have interactions with outside environments. Parts of the organizational system and the environment are in dynamic and ever-changing interaction. Managers must, therefore, understand and be able to work within this reality.

Putting together the three primary streams of management thought (classical, behavioral, quantitative) with the dynamic systems concept led to an obvious conclusion, which most managers understood through experience: there is no one way to manage. Such formal realization led to the development of contingency (situational) theory, which requires managers to understand organizational situations accurately and thoroughly, identify the important issues and variables in context, and develop courses of action that are appropriate to situational realities. Implicit in contingency theory is the idea that the insights provided by classical, behavioral, and quantitative approaches to management should all be understood and applied appropriately.

Quality, Strategy, and Diversity

Various new threads have entered the tapestry of management thought since the 1980s. The Quality Management movement (Total Quality Management) has enjoyed high visibility and taught (actually reminded) managers that doing things right the first time is better than doing things in ways that force organizations to continually correct mistakes.

Also, attention is now being directed to top-level (strategic) managers who are responsible for determining the nature, purpose, structure, function, and the future of the organization as a whole. Thus, increased attention is given to vision (what the organization is to become), mission (what the organization is about and what

The Uses of Qualitative Management

- Analyzing costs
- Optimizing decision outcomes
- Evaluating individual, group, machine, and system performance
- Simulating processes and decision outcomes
- Using probabilities to make decisions under conditions of uncertainty
- Assessing behaviors of competitors
- Managing inventories to minimize costs
- Planning and controlling complex projects
- Forecasting demand for products and services

it values), and strategy (the plan that employs the mission and directs the organization in ways to achieve the vision).

Finally, more attention is being given to the increased presence of, and opportunities for managing the reality of, more women and minorities in the workforce. These are not really new issues, but they do represent new awareness and socially important concerns.

Will management theory ever achieve integration and closure? Probably not. How to select, educate, and promote managers will always be a struggle, but the availability of a wide range of management theories should help society and will help people who aspire to and are chosen to manage. The challenge of being accountable for the performance of the people who work for them will ensure that managers will never be bored.

Further Reading

Fayol, Henri. *General and Industrial Management.* 1949. Reprint, New York: Institute of Electrical and Electronics Engineers, 1984.

Koontz, Harold, ed. *Toward a Unified Theory of Management.* New York: McGraw-Hill, 1964.

Koontz, Harold, and Heinz Weihrich. *Management.* 10th ed. New York: McGraw-Hill, 1993.

Matteson, Michael T., and John M. Ivancevich. *Management and Organizational Behavior Classics.* 6th ed. Chicago: Irwin, 1996.

Taylor, Frederick W. *The Principles of Scientific Management.* 1911. Reprint, Westport, Conn.: Greenwood Press, 1972.

Weber, Max. *Max Weber: The Theory of Social and Economic Organization.* Translated by A. M. Henderson and Talcott Parsons. New York: Free Press, 1964.

Wren, Daniel A. *The Evolution of Management Thought.* 4th ed. New York: John Wiley & Sons, 1994.

—*John Washbush*

Managers are increasingly called upon to confront issues of diversity in the workplace.

Manufacturing Industry

Manufacturing is best understood as the production of goods, usually in a factory. Manufacturers produce consumer goods as well as the materials and machines that make them—a litany of items that includes steel, automobiles, ships, paper, printing presses, textiles, clothing, chemicals, pharmaceuticals, food items, biotechnologies, electronics, and computers.

Some of the most robust economies in the world have been and are built upon a strong manufacturing base, beginning with Great Britain. The development of the steam engine in 1769 and the ensuing Industrial Revolution transformed Great Britain into the early leader in manufacturing. Indeed, Great Britain's textile industry was one of the first in which full-scale machines, for example, the spinning wheel and cotton gin, were used to boost human productivity. The Industrial Revolution spread to the United States, and by 1850 manufacturers in Great Britain had begun to emulate the American System of manufacturing, which was based on division of labor, mechanization, standardization, and interchangeable parts.

The American System

The American System (also known as the American Plan, the Springfield System, and the "almost perfect system of Samuel Colt") has roots in the production of small arms, guns and rifles, in the early nineteenth century. As early as 1801, Eli Whitney demonstrated the virtues of interchangeable parts in guns. However, scholars assert that the American System did not truly take shape for several decades, until gun production began at the first national armories, located in Harpers Ferry, Virginia, and Springfield, Massachusetts. The first main line production use of the American System occurred in 1840, at Samuel Colt's Springfield armory.

The American System manufacturing processes were supported by the U.S. Ordnance Department, which outlined in its arms contracts specifications for production, leading to increased uniformity, standardization, and interchangeability of parts. While Whitney had hand-filed gun parts to match production patterns, later manufacturers developed machine tools that ensured conformity in the parts. These machine tools revolutionized manufacturing. In 1851 British engineers observed such machine tools at London's Crystal Palace Exhibition, and the American System of manufacturing spread abroad.

In the United States, the American System spread from arms production to consumer industries. Isaac Singer, founder of the Singer Manufacturing Company, hired three machinists from the arms industry to develop his sewing machine production system. These manufacturing techniques helped Singer become the leading producer of sewing machines in the United States by the 1860s; Singer made 43,000 machines in 1867 alone. Well into the 1880s, however, Singer workers still hand-finished and fitted many of the machines, a practice that kept Singer from pushing manufacturing practices forward toward mass production. (According to the 1926 *Encyclopaedia Britannica* entry on mass production, "In mass production, there are no fitters.")

Soon, innumerable goods—including clocks, textile machinery, printing presses, locomotives, typewriters, and bicycles—were being produced by the tens and hundreds of thousands. In the 1890s, an era known for the bicycle boom, bicycle manufacturers made production processes even more efficient with new metalworking techniques, including sheet metal stamping and electric-resistance welding. These processes were later used in automobile manufacturing and helped usher in the assembly line.

Fordism

Henry Ford transformed manufacturing into mass production in 1914, with the development of the moving assembly lines at the Highland Park, Michigan, Ford plant. The advent of the assembly line marked the first time in history that goods could be produced in the millions. In addition to greater quantities, labor productivity increased tenfold, allowing the price of a Model T to drop from $780 in 1910 to $360 in 1914. By 1924 Ford's company had produced more than 2,000,000 cars, up from 300,000 in 1914, and the company held more than 50 percent of the U.S. car market.

Ford's manufacturing plants were arguably the most prolific in the world and, as his technique for mass production spread to other industries, it was dubbed "Fordism." As a manufacturing concept, Fordism was marked by a moving assembly line and minute divisions of labor. This enabled a highly mechanized, steady flow of production that created uniform commodities in high volume. Ford also instituted the $5 per day wage, nearly doubling the wages of most automobile factory workers at the time, and cut working hours by 40 percent. Both measures were intended to offset the high turnover rate of employees caused by the quick-paced, physically taxing, repetitive, and often boring work.

As early as 1926, however, Ford's production methods were becoming obsolete. By the 1930s, General Motors (GM) had taken the lead in mass production. GM's system also relied on the moving assembly line and division of labor, but it emphasized the interchangeability of workers, as well as parts. The GM system strove to simplify manufacturing activities as much as possible—separating production, engineering, management, and administrative functions—and placed the

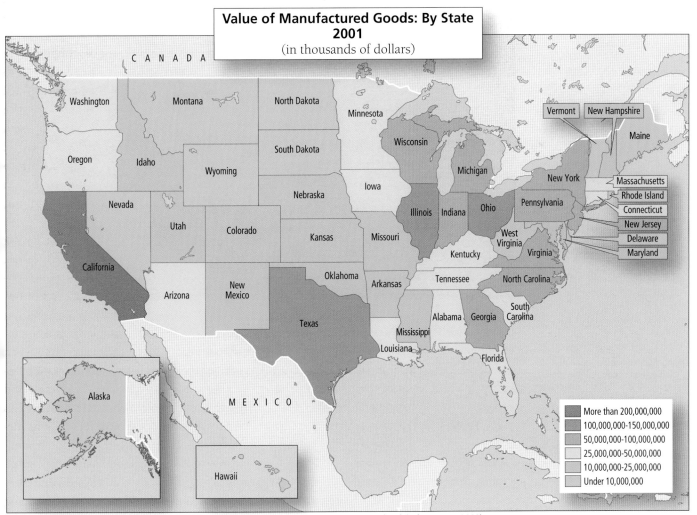

Value of Manufactured Goods: By State 2001
(in thousands of dollars)

More than 200,000,000
100,000,000-150,000,000
50,000,000-100,000,000
25,000,000-50,000,000
10,000,000-25,000,000
Under 10,000,000

Source: U.S. Bureau of the Census, *2002 Economic Census,* http://www.census.gov/mcd/asmhome.html (February 12, 2003).

Smelting steel in an Iowa plant.

power to command in the hands of a small, central managing body. This top-down hierarchical structure quickly penetrated most industries and helped the United States become the world's dominant economic force in the 1950s.

Japanization and the Toyota Production System

Just as Ford's advance in the automobile industry transformed nearly all manufacturing from the 1920s on, Japan's leading automobile manufacturing technology, the Toyota Production System (TPS), has revolutionized manufacturing worldwide. The founder of Toyota's automobile manufacturing division, Eiji Toyoda, visited Ford's factories in the 1930s and then adapted Fordism to suit Japan's production culture. Manufacturers of goods ranging from clothing to computer chips are intimately familiar with the hallmarks of TPS, which include total quality management (TQM) and just-in-time delivery (JIT). TPS is also referred to as "Japanization," "flexible production," and "lean production."

The core of TPS is the elimination of waste at all levels of production, from streamlining physical production—for example, reducing unnecessary movements by assembly workers—to removing layers of excess managerial bureaucracy. Another aspect of TPS is valuing the intellectual capacities of assembly line workers as much as their physical capacities, based on the belief that workers know best how to improve production techniques. Through technological advances, many of the most repetitive and physically laborious tasks were mechanized. The role of the worker became more focused on supervising the machine's production for quality— a method called "autonomation" in Japan.

TPS also pioneered the efficient use of resources, low inventories, and JIT production and delivery practices.

Like Fordism, Japanization is marked by high stress and a blisteringly fast work pace. Indeed, Japanese factory workers log between 200 and 500 more hours than their American and European counterparts. Still, companies across the globe have adopted and adapted TPS manufacturing techniques, which have resulted in lower-cost goods and smaller, more efficient production facilities.

Global Manufacturing

As TPS spread during the 1980s and 1990s, so did global manufacturing. Since 1982 more than 1,275 Japanese "trans-plants" have established manufacturing operations in the United States, including car assembly plants, automotive suppliers, and steel and

Testing silicon wafers in Washington state.

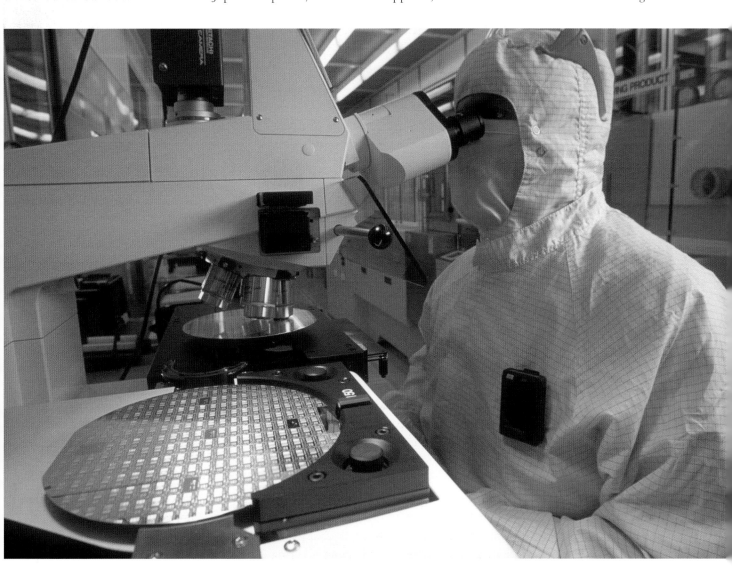

Careers in Manufacturing

An abundance of manufacturing jobs are available to people with varying levels of education and skill. Highly skilled workers in the industry include scientists and engineers who complete the research necessary before any product can be designed. Those careers often require advanced degrees. Other skilled workers often operate the machinery used to make a finished product. Those careers include machinists, engravers, and printers. Many workers attend technical and trade schools to learn the specific task. Less-skilled workers are more likely to work on projects that require repeated motions like packing, sorting, and moving equipment.

Finally, many people who work in the manufacturing industry manage other workers. In some cases, a worker earns the privilege of managing others after years of service. In other instances, a manager with an advanced degree is hired from outside the company.

Many manufacturing jobs have on-the-job training so employees can acquire skills once they have been hired and do not necessarily need experience for employment. Employees in manufacturing also receive extensive safety training once they begin work.

—Karen Ehrle

tire plants. As with Fordism and TPS, the move toward global manufacturing in the automobile industry also opened the doors for other industries. However, far from heralding a golden age of manufacturing, the move toward globalization took place as manufacturing in the most industrialized nations was in decline.

Manufacturing's percentage of America's gross domestic product (GDP) began to drop as early as the late 1950s. In Japan, a similar decline began in the early 1970s. Theorists proclaimed that the United States, Japan, and European manufacturing economies were moving into a postindustrial phase, with an emphasis on information and service over production of goods. Some even predicted the death of manufacturing. Between January 2002 and January 2003, manufacturing output in the United Kingdom dropped by 5.5 percent, in Germany by 5 percent, in the United States by 6 percent, and in Japan by 14 percent. At the same time, classic "hard" industries like steel production employed fewer and fewer workers because of restructuring and advances in automation. Job shortages were further exacerbated by the movement of labor-intensive manufacturing, especially in the textile industries, to low-wage countries with relatively poor working conditions. Indeed, many blue-collar jobs are disappearing as advanced manufacturing

processes reduce the need for low-skilled line workers, replacing them with machines and with more highly trained workers usually associated with white-collar, clerical, and administration positions.

Nevertheless, certain manufacturing industries still thrive. The automobile manufacturing industry remains the backbone of Germany's export economy, and in the United States it provides 20 percent of all manufacturing employment as well as most of the high-wage blue-collar jobs. In textiles and the garment industry, even as their traditional labor-intensive aspects falter, the high-tech end of textiles, in which synthetics are produced, has flourished. Similarly, new steels are developed every year.

Some observers argue that it is far too soon to declare manufacturing dead. They point out that goods remain more appealing than services, especially to the vast majority of the global population, which is poor. According to this line of thinking, a market for manufactured goods will always exist as well as a demand for manufacturing techniques and processes that are more efficient, less expensive, and use cheaper and more abundant materials.

Further Reading

Fingleton, Eamonn. *In Praise of Hard Industries: Why Manufacturing, Not the Information Economy, Is the Key to Future Prosperity.* Boston: Houghton Mifflin, 1999.

Hounshell, David A. *From the American System to Mass Production, 1800–1932: The Development of Manufacturing Technology in the United States.* Baltimore, Md.: Johns Hopkins University Press, 1984.

Kenney, Martin, and Richard Florida. *Beyond Mass Production: The Japanese System and Its Transfer to the U.S.* New York: Oxford University Press, 1993.

Maynard, Micheline. *The Global Manufacturing Vanguard: New Rules from the Industry Elite.* New York: John Wiley & Sons, 1998.

Timmer, Marcel P. *The Dynamics of Asian Manufacturing.* Cheltenham, U.K.: Edward Elgar, 2000.

Womack, James, Daniel T. Jones, and Daniel Roos. *The Machine That Changed the World.* New York: HarperPerennial, 1991.

—Laura Lambert

Market Research

Somewhere between science and psychology lies market research. The objective of market research is to gain an understanding of customers in an attempt to sell them products or services. Although many business owners would like market research to be a science, the unpredictable human elements of preference and circumstance factor into every marketing formula ever designed. The buying public's fancy is not always predictable.

The science component of market research takes into account demographics: age, income, race, occupation, and level of education. The psychology component, called psychographics, relates to lifestyle. Market researchers look at where people live, both address and kind of residence. They track where they are in their life cycle—single, just married, newly pregnant, retired. They also study changing roles in the home, for example, who cooks and who shops. Lifestyle can also be more general in nature, including trends toward healthier living, later marriages, and fewer children. Psychographic variables make conducting completely accurate market research impossible, but companies strive to learn as much as possible about people and their lifestyles so they can make smart business decisions.

Early Market Research

The first American market researcher is generally considered to be Charles Coolidge Parlin. In 1910 he did research for the Curtis Publishing Company. His mission was to gather information that might be helpful to businesses that advertised in the company's numerous magazines. His information allowed advertisers to fine-tune their marketing plans to fit each magazine's readership and make better use of their advertising dollars.

Many companies, Coca-Cola and the Chicago Tribune among them, followed suit with their own versions of market research. By the 1920s the field of market research blossomed. It also began a subtle shift in emphasis. In the early days, market research was based on function: how to get goods to people who were geographically dispersed. As companies began to fear market saturation for their products, they changed focus from function to style. Instead of worrying about how to get products to people, they strove to figure out how to get people to buy more products. For example, General Motors responded to the fear of market saturation by changing the style of its cars every year beginning in 1927. The purpose was to create dissatisfaction in the consumer: "I have an old style of car, and I want the newer [implicitly better] style of car." GM used market research to both find and create that dissatisfaction.

The mass popularity of radio in the mid-1920s changed market research, and the television boom of the 1950s changed it further still. The idea of the mass market was born with the widespread coverage made possible by radio and television. Because companies could no longer take the people's purchasing pulse directly, they began using a relatively new technique for

See also:
Advertising, Business Practice; Advertising Industry; Consumerism; Credit History; Public Relations and Marketing, Business Practice.

Ways of Conducting Market Research	
Type of Market Research	**Methodology**
Observation	Observe consumers; read trade publications; watch competition.
Face Time	Utilize focus groups; one-on-one interviews; questionnaires; product tests and demonstrations.
Personal Research	Research government, library and trade associations; collect information from company Web site.
Information Purchase	Purchase data from information brokers.

A sorting machine used by the U.S. Bureau of the Census, circa 1911. For many years the Census Bureau was the primary provider of market research data.

that time, scientific polling. Companies would ask people a series of questions, then tabulate the results to get a feel for their customers.

The Census Bureau

The technology needed to compile large amounts of market research came from a somewhat unexpected place. Oddly enough, it was inspired by a decree in the Constitution—that the United States should count its citizens every 10 years. In 1880 Herman Hollerith, an employee at the Bureau of the Census, designed and built a tabulating machine that used punch cards, metal pens, and electrical contacts to compile information. This machine, which was to become the forerunner of computer punch card systems, was used to tabulate the results of the 1890 census. Hollerith started his own company and, in 1911, merged it with three others to

form what would become International Business Machines, or IBM.

Around the same time, businesses began showing an interest in U.S. census data for their market research. The Census Bureau had subdivided the whole United States into census tracts (about 4,000 people) and then into census blocks (approximately 85 people in urban areas, 30 in rural areas). The bureau's purpose was to help the census takers as, at the time (and up until 1960), all data gathering was done in person. The bureau's subdivisions, coupled with Hollerith's tabulating machine, made possible the tabulating of census data in small pieces. Companies could now get a very specific look at the people they were selling to. Having a little information increased companies' desire to know more.

By 1951 the Census Bureau had begun using the world's first commercial digital computer, called the Universal Automatic Computer (UNIVAC). It too used punch cards, but the data were registered on magnetic tape that could be used to create custom reports of the census information. Although the UNIVAC arrived too late for the 1950 census, the computer was used to compile almost all of the 1960 census data. A few years after the census, though still early in the computer revolution, companies gained access to computers that had enough speed and memory to manipulate and analyze the numbers from the census. At that point, the U.S. Census Bureau became more than a government agency that counted people. It began to sell its data to commercial concerns. In 1963 the then–Post Office began using zip codes, giving companies yet another way to coordinate and analyze data in conjunction with the census data.

For many years the Census Bureau was a major supplier of market research data. The bureau still provides helpful information, especially for small businesses, but its role in market research has diminished because of the vast array of information available from other sources. Census information forms only a small part of what market research firms collect today.

Kinds of Market Research

Market research is the first step in creating a marketing plan. Good research methods collect both demographic and psychographic information, which can be used to identify potential new markets, increase market share, determine pricing, and support market segmentation analysis. Research is conducted in a number of ways: observation, "face time," personal research, and information purchase.

The least costly form of research is simple observation of what is going on in the marketplace. To stay profitable, companies must be aware of trends in the marketplace and must distinguish them from fads. A trend is a sustained interest in a product that lasts at least five to 10 years whereas a fad is a short-term interest in a product, usually one to two years. Reading trade publications or simply seeing what people are buying and doing can alert researchers to trends. Another way to spot trends is to watch the competition. What subtle shifts are other companies making to adjust to the market? Are they offering new products, advertising in a new area, promoting a new color? Changes may point to a new trend.

A huge part of market research includes "face time"—time spent talking to the customer base face-to-face, for example, in focus groups, one-on-one interviews, questionnaires, or product tests and demonstrations. This kind of market research is either qualitative or quantitative. Qualitative research involves a free flow of ideas between the consumer and the researcher. This kind of interaction typically happens during a focus group or a personal interview. Questions are open-ended and the researcher encourages a certain amount of antagonism toward the product, needing the bad news as well as the good. Qualitative analysis helps the researcher identify the customer and the customer's concerns.

Some market research is conducted by telephone, with operators calling people to ask their opinions on different products, companies, or issues.

Quantitative research is more structured. Questionnaires are the best example. The questionnaire should be designed to test the validity of the conclusions drawn from the earlier qualitative analysis. The questions should lead to very specific answers, either enforcing or destroying the researcher's earlier conclusions.

Prototypes and test markets are used to get both qualitative and quantitative information. A prototype is a working model of a product. Consumers can respond in an informal way or by answering specific questions. Test markets, small geographic areas used to test new products alongside the competition, provide valuable insight into how the products measure up in the real world.

Personal research is research that a company conducts on its own, as opposed to information purchase, which is research a company buys. A variety of resources can be used for personal research, starting with a public or college library and trade associations. The government provides a wealth of research material through the Department of Commerce, Small Business Administration, chambers of commerce, and of course, the Census Bureau. If a company has a Web site, it can track each visitor's activity on the site through "cookies," bits of encrypted information deposited on a computer's hard drive.

The key to market research is gathering useful information. When beginning a research project on its own, a company must know what kind of information it is looking for and how it plans to use it. Using all these resources is time consuming, but the investment in research gives companies an edge over their competition.

Information Brokers

One popular method of conducting market research is to purchase the needed research from companies that specialize in gathering information and analyzing and combining it in any number of ways. One company, Metromail, keeps a database that compiles information from 3,500 sources.

The first places to look for information on individuals and households are usually state, local, and national public records, including those of the Census Bureau. For example, all real estate transactions are a matter of public record, so a research company can get a lot of information from a single transaction: names, addresses, income, price paid for the home, property assessment, amount of down payment, and more. State Departments of Motor Vehicles have information on driving records, what kind of car a person drives, and its value. Those two sources alone tell a lot about people: where they live and what they drive often speak volumes about their preferred lifestyle.

Credit bureaus collect and sell information about people, including income, number of credit lines, and legal obligations related to money. They typically know marital status, number of children, and other personal information gleaned from credit applications. They also collect information from creditors and landlords about payment history on a monthly basis. Credit bureaus are major sources of information for data collectors.

Pros and Cons of Information Brokers	
Pros	**Cons**
• Information available quickly	• Data may not address specific question
• Cost modest	• Answers may lack specificity
• Information objective	• Data may not be comparable with other sources
• May be only source of specific data	• Quality varies
• Improves focus of additional research	• Information may be dated

Source: Edward F. McQuarrie, *The Market Research Toolbox: A Concise Guide for Beginners,* Thousand Oaks, Calif., Sage Publications, 1996.

Smaller sources of information are also available. Catalog companies can track who their catalogs go to and which customers buy, then document that information and sell it to others. Magazine companies sell their subscription lists with whatever information they have accumulated. Rebate offers are a way of identifying the segment of the market that responds to such offers. The list of those consumers can be sold to companies that seek coupon and rebate redeemers. A general rule is that any time a customer deals with a company by filling out a form of any kind, unless that company specifically states otherwise, any information shared should be considered as available to be sold in the information market.

Businesses can purchase lists from list companies that identify potential customers, who can then be targeted for specific kinds of advertising and specific products. One kind of target marketing is life-cycle marketing. Companies identify people who are at a particular stage of life, then send them the appropriate advertisements and marketing materials. For example, a pregnant woman would be a target for offers involving formula, diapers, nursing pads, and so on. Singles are targets for dating services. Seniors are targets for life insurance, leisure activities, and health aids.

Is moving often a good way to escape the list companies? Only if no forwarding address is left with the United States Postal Service, which provides forwarding address services to the list companies because advertising ("junk") mail provides a large portion of its revenues. If the post office did not sell forwarding information, many consumers would be lost in the shuffle.

Many people are surprised to find just how much personal information is available to whomever wishes to pay for it. To some it may seem reminiscent of George Orwell's *1984*, in which mind police could get into people's brains to know what they were thinking—violating their privacy the way marketing research firms try to do with psychographic studies. However, many people have such busy lives that they thrive on convenience—frozen foods, drive-through drug stores, or ordering goods over the Internet at any time of day. All

this convenience and product improvement owe a great deal to the wealth of data accumulated through market research.

Further Reading

Hague, Paul, and Peter Jackson. *Market Research: A Guide to Planning, Methodology and Evaluation.* 2nd ed. London: Kogan Page, 1999.

Hall, John A. *Bringing New Products to Market: The Art and Science of Creating Winners.* New York: AMACOM, 1991.

Larson, Erik. *The Naked Consumer: How Our Private Lives Become Public Commodities.* New York: Henry Holt, 1992.

McQuarrie, Edward F. *The Market Research Toolbox: A Concise Guide for Beginners.* Thousand Oaks, Calif.: Sage Publications, 1996.

Pinson, Linda, and Jerry Jinnett. *Target Marketing for the Small Business: Researching, Reaching and Retaining Your Target Market.* 3rd ed. Chicago: Upstart Publishing Company, 1996.

—*Stephanie Buckwalter*

The president of Research & Polling, Inc., looks at research data at his office in Albuquerque, New Mexico, in 2002.

See also:
Capitalism; Communism;
Socialism.

Marx, Karl

1818–1883
Philosopher

The German economist, philosopher, and revolutionary Karl Marx is the acknowledged founder of modern communism. In the twentieth century his ideas inspired communist revolutions in Russia, China, Eastern Europe, and many postcolonial countries in Africa, Asia, Latin America, and the Caribbean.

Marx was born in the Prussian city of Trier (now part of Germany) to Jewish parents who had converted to Christianity to escape anti-Semitic laws. He was educated at Bonn and Berlin universities and received his doctorate in classical philosophy. As a student, he became prominent among the liberal Young Hegelians, followers of the idealist philosophy of G. W. F. Hegel, who emphasized the power of ideas to shape the material world. Because of his critiques of the Prussian government, Marx was denied a university teaching position. He then moved into political journalism and edited a liberal newspaper in Cologne, until it was suppressed by the government. In 1843 he married Jenny von Westphalen and they moved to Paris, where he became interested in French socialism. In his *Economic and Philosophic Manuscripts* (1844) Marx set out his emerging communist critique of the capitalist system. That same year, he met Friedrich Engels, his collaborator and benefactor for the rest of his life.

Toward the end of 1844, Marx and Engels were expelled from Paris for their political activities, and they settled in Brussels. Marx immersed himself in study and moved away from his early interest in Hegelian idealism, turning instead to the study of philosophical materialism, according to which ideas are shaped by conditions in the physical world. The study of materialism strengthened his conviction that philosophy should always be connected to practical political activity. In his *Theses on Feuerbach* (1845), Marx wrote the words that serve as his epitaph: "Philosophers have only interpreted the world in various ways; the point, however, is to change it." Similarly, when the French anarchist Pierre-Joseph Proudhon published *The Philosophy of Poverty* (1846), Marx wrote a blistering reply, *The Poverty of Philosophy* (1847).

In *The German Ideology* (1846) Marx first set out his materialist analysis of society as a product of economic factors. At this time, he also became active in the Communist League, for which he and Engels wrote *The Communist Manifesto* (1848). The *Manifesto*, which was completed after Marx was living in exile in London, contended that all history is the story of struggle between opposing classes, that history would culminate in a communist-led revolution of the workers against the capitalist system, and that capitalism would be superseded by a communist society founded upon the principles of full human equality and the common ownership of property.

In early 1848, as several democratic revolutions erupted in Europe, Marx continued

1818
Karl Marx
born.

1844
Marx meets
Friedrich Engels.

1848
Marx and Engels publish
The Communist Manifesto.

Karl Marx

1864
Marx cofounds the
First International.

1867
Marx publishes the first
volume of *Capital.*

1883
Marx dies.

his political activities in France and Germany; he then moved to London, where he was to live in exile for the rest of his life. He and his growing family lived in squalor, supported mainly by Engels, whose family owned a successful cotton business in Manchester, England. Marx also earned some money as a journalist, serving as a foreign correspondent for the *New York Daily Tribune*. Poverty took its toll on Marx and his family. Several of his children died very young; he would survive both his wife and his eldest daughter.

Despite his poor living conditions, Marx read and wrote prolifically. In *The Class Struggles in France* (1850) and *The Eighteenth Brumaire of Louis Bonaparte* (1852), he analyzed what he described as the bourgeois, or capitalist, revolutions of 1848. He became convinced that the communist revolution would be triggered by a capitalist economic crisis, so he committed himself to a rigorous study of political economy in the library of the British Museum. He set out his preliminary thoughts in *Grundrisse* (Outlines) (1858), and nine years later he published the first volume of his monumental *Capital* (1867). This was the work in which Marx explained, in technical economic detail, his theories of capitalist exploitation.

The progress of Marx's economic writings was slowed by his political activities on behalf of the communist International Workingman's Association, also known as the First International, which Marx had helped found in 1864. Until the early 1870s, Marx was preoccupied with his ultimately successful efforts to prevent the anarchists, led by Mikhail Bakunin, from taking over the International. This infighting severely weakened the International, which went into terminal decline and was eventually disbanded in 1876.

In 1871, in the wake of the Franco–Prussian War, the citizens of Paris took control of the city in what became known as the Paris Commune. When French troops crushed this political experiment after two months, Marx wrote *The Civil War in France*

(1871), the last of his great political pamphlets, in which he defended the Commune as an authentic working-class revolution. The experience of the French Communards strengthened Marx's view on the need for an uncompromising revolutionary party. In *The Critique of the Gotha Program* (1875), Marx urged the German communists not to merge with the mainstream socialists, and he offered his famous definition of a communist society as one based on the principle of "from each according to his ability, to each according to his needs."

Economist and philosopher Karl Marx (undated portrait).

The Communist Manifesto
(Excerpt)

[T]he theory of the Communists may be summed up in the single sentence: Abolition of private property.

We Communists have been reproached with the desire of abolishing the right of personally acquiring property as the fruit of a man's own labor, which property is alleged to be the groundwork of all personal freedom, activity, and independence.

Hard-won, self acquired, self-earned property! Do you mean the property of petty artisan and of the small peasant, a form of property that preceded the bourgeois form? There is no need to abolish that; the development of industry has to a great extent already destroyed it, and is still destroying it daily.

Or do you mean the modern bourgeois private property?

But does wage labor create any property for the laborer? Not a bit. It creates capital, i.e., that kind of property which exploits wage labor, and which cannot increase except upon conditions of begetting a new supply of wage labor for fresh exploitation. Property, in its present form, is based on the antagonism of capital and wage labor. . . .

And the abolition of this state of things is called by the bourgeois, abolition of individuality and freedom! And rightly so. The abolition of bourgeois individuality, bourgeois independence, and bourgeois freedom is undoubtedly aimed at.

By freedom is meant, under the present bourgeois conditions of production, free trade, free selling and buying.

But if selling and buying disappears, free selling and buying disappears also. This talk about free selling and buying, and all the other "brave words" of our bourgeois about freedom in general, have a meaning, if any, only in contrast with restricted selling and buying, with the fettered traders of the Middle Ages, but have no meaning when opposed to the communist abolition of buying and selling, or the bourgeois conditions of production, and of the bourgeoisie itself.

You are horrified at our intending to do away with private property. But in your existing society, private property is already done away with for nine-tenths of the population; its existence for the few is solely due to its non-existence in the hands of those nine-tenths. You reproach us, therefore, with intending to do away with a form of property, the necessary condition for whose existence is the non-existence of any property for the immense majority of society.

In one word, you reproach us with intending to do away with your property. Precisely so; that is just what we intend.

From the moment when labor can no longer be converted into capital, money, or rent, into a social power capable of being monopolized, i.e., from the moment when individual property can no longer be transformed into bourgeois property, into capital, from that moment, you say, individuality vanishes.

You must, therefore, confess that by "individual" you mean no other person than the bourgeois, than the middle-class owner of property. This person must, indeed, be swept out of the way, and made impossible.

Communism deprives no man of the power to appropriate the products of society; all that it does is to deprive him of the power to subjugate the labor of others by means of such appropriations.

For the remainder of his life, Marx's productivity as a writer and an activist was seriously hindered by his deteriorating health. He died on March 13, 1883. Engels completed the remaining two volumes of *Capital*, working from Marx's research notes.

In his lifetime, Marx's influence was limited. His works were not widely read, and he was not a charismatic personality or orator. Insofar as he had disciples, he quarreled with their interpretation of his ideas, once writing to Engels that "All I know is that I am not a Marxist." Few political thinkers, however, have had such a profound impact on the course of history. The implosion of communist systems in the years following 1989 has greatly diminished the stature of Marxism as a political movement, but many of its theoretical concepts still influence scholarly work in philosophy and the social sciences.

Further Reading

Berlin, Isaiah. *Karl Marx: His Life and Environment*. 4th ed. New York: Oxford University Press, 1996.

Marx, Karl. *Karl Marx: Selected Writings*. Edited by David McLellan. 2nd ed. Oxford: Oxford University Press, 2000.

Marx, Karl, and Friedrich Engels. *The Communist Manifesto*. Edited by David McLellan. Oxford: Oxford University Press, 1992.

Rius, Tom Engelhardt, ed. *Marx for Beginners*. New York: Pantheon, 1979.

Wheen, Francis. *Karl Marx: A Life*. New York: W. W. Norton, 2000.

—*Peter C. Grosvenor*

Master of Business Administration

The master of business administration (MBA) is the postgraduate, professional degree that offers preparation for high-level management positions in business. Students who earn the MBA most frequently pursue careers with for-profit firms. However, MBA programs develop leadership, analytic, and decision-making skills that are also applicable in the nonprofit and governmental sectors.

The Association to Advance Collegiate Schools of Business (AACSB) was organized in 1916 to promote and improve higher education in business administration and management. The AACSB has accredited more than 400 MBA programs in the United States, Canada, and Mexico as well as others outside North America. Institutions that offer graduate business education include the London Business School, INSEAD in France and Singapore, the International Graduate School of Management in Spain, and the International Institute of Management Development in Switzerland.

Most MBA programs require two academic years of class work. In the first year, students take core courses that provide a foundation in economics, marketing, finance, accounting, management, and statistical analysis. During the second year, students focus on a specific business area of interest, or avail themselves of niche programs in areas like entrepreneurship, e-commerce, or supply chain management. In addition to course content, MBA programs strive to foster an appreciation for group effort and to develop the leadership skills necessary to assure success in the business world. Throughout the two years, group projects and team-building exercises are common, with some schools demanding that incoming students work with the same peer group during their entire first year.

Reflecting the growing importance of global business operations, MBA programs have worked to internationalize their curriculums. In addition to courses that focus on global business topics, many U.S. schools offer study trips, semester-long exchanges with universities outside the United States, and opportunities to participate in team consulting projects abroad. A number of schools, including Duke University and the University of Chicago, have established campuses outside the United States.

Graduate business education began at major U.S. universities during the early decades of the twentieth century, and, in the 1920s, the Harvard Business School introduced the case study as a means of incorporating actual business problems into class work. Designed to improve decision-making skills, a case, which can be relatively short

See also:
Education Industry;
Entrepreneurship.

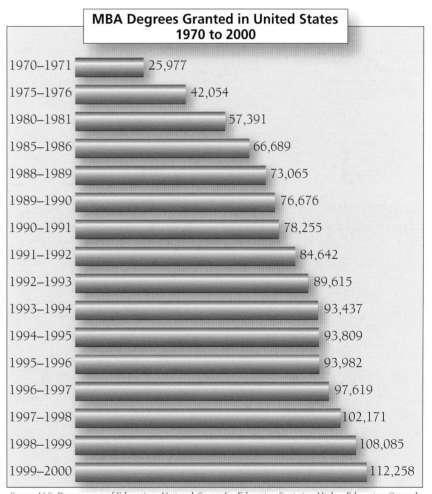

MBA Degrees Granted in United States 1970 to 2000

Year	Degrees
1970–1971	25,977
1975–1976	42,054
1980–1981	57,391
1985–1986	66,689
1988–1989	73,065
1989–1990	76,676
1990–1991	78,255
1991–1992	84,642
1992–1993	89,615
1993–1994	93,437
1994–1995	93,809
1995–1996	93,982
1996–1997	97,619
1997–1998	102,171
1998–1999	108,085
1999–2000	112,258

Source: U.S. Department of Education, National Center for Education Statistics, Higher Education General Information Survey (HEGIS); "Degrees and Other Formal Awards Conferred" surveys; and Integrated Postsecondary Education Data System "Completions" surveys, 2001.

Some MBA Majors and Fields of Study

- Accounting
- Arts management
- Corporate finance
- Educational administration
- Electronic commerce
- Entrepreneurial management
- Environmental management
- Finance
- Government
- Health care administration
- Human resources
- Information management
- International finance
- International policy
- Investment management
- Manufacturing management
- Marketing
- Multinational management
- Nonprofit organizations
- Operations management
- Public finance
- Real estate
- Small business management
- Strategic management
- Urban finance and development

BusinessWeek's Top 30 MBA Programs in the United States 2002

1	Northwestern (Kellogg)	16	UCLA (Anderson)
2	Chicago	17	USC (Marshall)
3	Harvard	18	UNC (Kenan-Flagler)
4	Stanford	19	Carnegie Mellon
5	Pennsylvania (Wharton)	20	Indiana (Kelley)
6	MIT (Sloan)	21	Texas (McCombs)
7	Columbia	22	Emory (Goizueta)
8	Michigan	23	Michigan State
9	Duke (Fuqua)	24	Washington (Olin)
10	Dartmouth (Tuck)	25	Maryland (Smith)
11	Cornell (Johnson)	26	Purdue (Krannert)
12	Virginia (Darden)	27	Rochester (Simon)
13	UC Berkeley (Haas)	28	Vanderbilt (Owen)
14	Yale	29	Notre Dame (Mendoza)
15	NYU (Stern)	30	Georgetown (McDonough)

Source: BusinessWeek, McGraw-Hill Companies, 2002. Used with permission.

or more than 20 pages, provides extensive information regarding a specific management issue confronting a firm. Prior to class meetings, student teams read and prepare possible solutions to the problems presented in the case. Then, led by the course instructor, they engage in intense class discussions that probe the particular circumstances associated with the business problem, analyze the advantages and disadvantages of alternative solutions to the problem, and reach a final decision about the firm's optimal course of action.

The so-called case method accounts for about 80 percent of the instruction at the Harvard Business School. To a lesser extent, most other MBA programs in the United States and abroad also use case study as a pedagogical tool. In addition, other instruction methods, including computer-based simulations and group projects, have gained widespread acceptance in the MBA curriculum. Many schools encourage students to expand their "real world" experience with a business internship during the summer following the first year of graduate training.

All accredited MBA programs require applicants to take the Graduate Management Admissions Test (GMAT). The test is composed of verbal and quantitative multiple-choice sections and two essays. The 41 verbal questions assess the ability to comprehend and evaluate written material; the 37 quantitative questions test basic math knowledge, including algebra and geometry, as well as skill in interpreting data presented in graphs, tables, and charts. Two required essays measure ability to argue logically and to write in a concise, persuasive, and grammatically correct style. Possible scores on the GMAT range from 200 to 800; the average score is around 530.

On average, selected applicants at the top 30 MBA programs are in their late 20s, have four to five years of work experience (not necessarily in a business venue), and have GMAT scores above 600. Less prestigious schools enroll a higher percent of applicants, and they may accept younger students who have just finished their

undergraduate degrees, as well as older persons who have been in the workforce for many years. Such schools also require applicants to take the GMAT, but they may accept considerably lower scores.

In addition to full-time programs, graduate business schools have developed a number of alternatives to serve nontraditional students. The Executive MBA is an intensive course of study designed for higher-level executives with substantial work experience. Classes are held on weekends or evenings and are completed in a fraction of the time necessary for the traditional degree. Part-time MBA programs serve the needs of individuals who wish to obtain the degree and remain in the workforce. Students complete the same number of courses as those in full-time programs, but they schedule classes during evening or weekend hours and extend their course load over more semesters. The online MBA is the most recent innovation in graduate business education and is designed for students who need maximum flexibility. Depending on the school, students complete all or part of their course work using Internet technology.

The MBA is one of the most highly sought professional degrees. Thousands of applicants compete fiercely each year for a limited number of places in the entering classes of the top business schools. In 2000 the Wharton School at the University of Pennsylvania accepted 14 percent of applicants, the Kellogg School at Northwestern University accepted 18 percent, Harvard Business School accepted 13 percent, and the Sloan School at the Massachusetts Institute of Technology accepted 17 percent.

Further Reading

Gruber, Betsy, Margaret Littman, and Jennifer Merritt. *Business Week Guide to the Best Business Schools.* 7th ed. New York: McGraw-Hill, 2001.

Housman, Jon. *The MBA Jungle: B-School Survival Guide.* Cambridge, Mass.: Perseus Publishing, 2001.

—*Marilyn Lavin*

A class in management at the Harvard Business School in Cambridge, Massachusetts.

Mayer, Louis B.

1885–1957
Hollywood executive

Louis B. Mayer grew up in a family of struggling immigrants and rose to become the most prominent motion picture executive of the 1920s. Mayer's studio employed glamorous stars in spectacular films that thrilled the first generation of movie fans.

Born Eliezer Mayer in 1885 in Minsk, Russia, Louis immigrated to the Americas as a toddler with his mother, father, and two older sisters. Settling first in New York, Louis's father, Jacob, worked as a peddler, hawking discarded bottles, old tin cans, and other scraps along the dirty streets of Manhattan. The Mayers soon abandoned big city squalor in favor of small-town life in St. John, Canada. Young Louis played baseball and made friends with children of local businessmen, including the son of the local theater owner, who gave Louis discounted admissions. Mayer later recalled being dazzled by that theater from the start.

Mayer graduated from high school in 1902. Following their traditions, the family arranged for his marriage. The woman of choice was Margaret, a curly-haired daughter of a kosher butcher in Boston. Shown a photograph, Louis liked what he saw and set off for Massachusetts to be wed.

Beginning with the skills he knew best, Louis gathered cotton waste and sold it for rags, packing, and mattresses. He moved on to develop a junk business, and then to the new craze that was sweeping the country: motion pictures. Mayer was quick to recognize the significance of films in American culture, noting that, for the first time, poor and uneducated people were able to enjoy the kind of professional entertainment previously reserved for those who could afford the high-priced tickets to live theater.

In 1907 Mayer took a chance and bought a run-down burlesque theater in Haverhill, Massachusetts. He persuaded friends and relatives to invest, and convinced employees to work temporarily without pay. His renovations restored the dilapidated building to its former beauty; Mayer showed only the highest-quality movies in that theater. In time, he owned New England's most influential group of theaters. Stunning, imaginative showpieces, his halls attracted thousands and were highly profitable.

His greatest achievement of that time was the gamble he took on a new and controversial film, *The Birth of a Nation* (1915).

Louis B. Mayer with actress Jean Harlow in 1933.

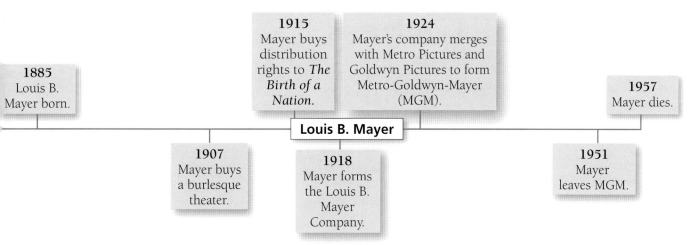

1885
Louis B. Mayer born.

1907
Mayer buys a burlesque theater.

1915
Mayer buys distribution rights to *The Birth of a Nation.*

Louis B. Mayer

1918
Mayer forms the Louis B. Mayer Company.

1924
Mayer's company merges with Metro Pictures and Goldwyn Pictures to form Metro-Goldwyn-Mayer (MGM).

1951
Mayer leaves MGM.

1957
Mayer dies.

Feeling sure the film would be a hit, Mayer claims to have gone so far as to pawn his wife's jewelry to buy sole New England distribution rights. That great risk returned $500,000 in profits, enough to bankroll Mayer in Hollywood. Mayer moved his wife and their three daughters to California, where he joined the fledgling film industry as an independent producer, forming the Louis B. Mayer Company in 1918. The company released primarily romantic melodramas starring actresses like Mildred Harris, Charlie Chaplin's estranged wife. In 1924 Mayer merged his company with Metro Pictures Corporation and Goldwyn Pictures Corporation, to create Metro-Goldwyn-Mayer (MGM).

Appointed vice president and general manager of productions, Mayer emerged as a powerful studio chief who ruled his "stable" with a big heart, a short temper, a loud voice, and a ruthlessly strong will. He treated his employees like children, telling them what to eat, what to wear, whom to marry, and when to have children. At the same time, he pampered them, insisting on first-class travel, reservations in the finest hotels, and cash advances from their salaries when they needed money for expensive clothes, houses, or cars. He assured them their appearance would be flawless; the camera never revealed, for instance, that Greta Garbo had fat ankles or that Clark Gable had false teeth.

Mayer went to great lengths to keep his stars spotless in the eyes of the public. In one instance, Mayer actually saved Gable's career. Driving drunk one night on Hollywood Boulevard, Gable killed a pedestrian. Mayer plotted with the local district attorney to have a movie executive charged with the crime instead. In return, the executive was given a higher salary for life, and Mayer managed to silence the press so that his star's image was saved.

Unlike other studios of the era, MGM stayed well away from controversial topics and risqué themes. During the Great Depression and World War II, Mayer felt the public would respond to his conservative tastes. MGM produced a huge number of classic films during Mayer's tenure, including *Ben Hur* (1925), *Dinner at Eight* (1933), and *Meet Me in St. Louis* (1944). Mayer was rewarded handsomely; at points during the 1930s and 1940s, Mayer's annual salary made him the highest paid person in the United States.

Mayer's way of getting the job done, through tyrannical leadership and exclusive contracts, worked well in his day, but times changed. Film stars sought independence and young executives sought power of their own. Mayer was forced from his position in 1951. He fought for the remaining years of his life in a futile attempt to return to power and died in 1957 of complications of leukemia.

Further Reading

Altman, Diana. *Hollywood East: Louis B. Mayer and the Origins of the Studio System.* New York: Carol Publishing, 1992.

Higham, Charles. *Merchant of Dreams: Louis B. Mayer, M.G.M., and the Secret Hollywood.* New York: Donald I. Fine, 1993.

—*Karen Ehrle*

McDonald's

Once known for its basic menu of burgers and fries, McDonald's has established itself as a leader of the U.S. fast-food industry, with its signature golden arches increasingly common in other parts of the world as well. McDonald's serves snacks and meals to millions of people daily; it employs legions of young people, providing many of them with their first jobs; and it has generated an array of competitors eager to develop their own applications of the ideas underlying McDonald's success.

The McDonald's story begins with Maurice and Richard McDonald, who moved from New Hampshire to California in the 1930s and opened their first restaurant, in Pasadena, in 1937. This restaurant was a conventional diner, serving no hamburgers. In 1940 the brothers opened a drive-in hamburger stand in a 600-square-foot building on the corner of 14th and E Streets in San Bernardino, California—at the terminus for fabled Route 66, at that time still a major artery into California.

The drive-in did a good business, but before long the McDonalds had a new idea. In 1948 they closed the restaurant for three months and renovated it. They threw out the restaurant china and silverware, reduced the menu to seven items (hamburgers, cheeseburgers, pie, potato chips, coffee, milk, and soda), got rid of the carhops, and reopened with a new mode of operation. Now the customers would come to a service window to collect their food, and they would receive ketchup, onions, mustard, and pickles automatically on every burger. Hamburgers were small, at 10 to a pound, but each burger cost only 15 cents.

McDonald's earlier customers reportedly detested the new concept, but the low prices and high quality of items offered on the new menu soon attracted families to the restaurant, and business grew rapidly (especially after the menu was augmented by french fries and milk shakes). As sales increased, the McDonald brothers continued to innovate,

inventing (together with a local machine shop owner, Ed Toman) almost everything now associated with fast-food service—dispensers to dole out precise amounts of ketchup and mustard, for example, and revolving trays that allowed up to 20 hamburger buns to be loaded with condiments in just a few seconds. They also introduced an assembly line of sorts, on which some people cooked the burgers, others fried the fries, and others made the shakes, so that food servings could be prepared in advance and dispensed quickly.

As early as 1950 the brothers posted a sign outside their restaurant announcing "over 1 million sold." By 1952 McDonald's

McDonald's

1937
Maurice and Richard McDonald open first restaurant in Pasadena, California.

1948
McDonald brothers remodel restaurant for faster service.

1955
Ray Kroc opens first McDonald's franchise.

1961
Kroc buys rights to McDonald's concept for $2.7 million.

1963
Ronald McDonald is introduced.

1965
McDonald's goes public.

1998
$2,250 worth of McDonald's stock bought in 1965 would be worth more than $2.8 million.

had become a legend in the food service industry, with annual sales of $350,000 and strong profits. It was featured on the cover of *American Restaurant* magazine. Owners of other restaurants visited frequently, wanting to know how McDonald's did it.

One of those who visited was Ray Kroc, a distributor of the Multimix milk shake mixers in use at McDonald's. Kroc was curious about the small hamburger stand—why was it using eight of his largest Multimixers, enough to make 40 milk shakes at one time? Kroc was impressed by what he saw. Although he was 52 years old and a successful Multimix distributor, he proposed an ambitious franchising plan by which he would become a partner with the McDonalds, chiefly responsible for establishing McDonald's restaurants throughout the United States. The McDonalds agreed, and Kroc opened the first McDonald's franchise in Des Plaines, Illinois, in 1955. By 1959 the number had increased to 100; by 1961, when Kroc bought the rights to the McDonald's concept for $2.7 million, the number of McDonald's restaurants had reached 200.

From this time on the business grew at an almost frantic pace. McDonald's was opening franchises so quickly that the company began Hamburger University to train franchisees. More than 500 people had graduated from Hamburger U by 1963, the year in which McDonald's neon signs first read, "more than 1 billion sold." Instruction at Hamburger U is now provided in 22 languages; more than 65,000 trainees have completed its program. McDonald's also provides management training at centers in England, Japan, Germany, and Australia.

The year 1963 also saw the opening of McDonald's five-hundredth restaurant and the debut of Ronald McDonald, the clown who would soon become a well-known McDonald's symbol. Within six years of appearing in his first national TV ad in 1965, Ronald McDonald was familiar to 96 percent of American children, more than knew the name of the president of the United States. His popularity was important to the company, as children's preferences often determined where families ate out.

In 1965 McDonald's went public with the company's first offering of shares for

This replica of the first corporate McDonald's restaurant, opened in Des Plaines, Illinois, in 1955, is actually the McDonald's Museum.

Russians line up to enter a newly opened McDonald's on Gorky Street in Moscow in 1990.

sale on the stock exchange. One hundred shares of stock, costing $2,250 on the first day of sales, had multiplied into 74,360 shares, worth more than $2.8 million, by the end of 1998.

What accounts for McDonald's success? One factor is consistency. McDonald's burgers and fries in California taste like McDonald's burgers and fries in South Carolina. Weary drivers stopping for coffee on a road trip often pull in at McDonald's, knowing that they will get similar coffee at any McDonald's. Another factor is responsiveness to evolving customer preferences—franchisees know their local territory. The Big Mac was invented and named by Jim Delligattia, a franchisee in Pittsburgh; the Fillet-o-Fish was thought up by a franchisee in a Roman Catholic section of Cincinnati, who wanted something to offer customers on Fridays; the Egg McMuffin was developed by a franchisee in Santa Barbara to compete with an eggs Benedict breakfast roll sold by rival Jack-in-the-Box.

In an average year, 96 percent of U.S. restaurant goers will eat at a McDonald's. The company buys more beef and potatoes, and trains more people, than any

other organization in the United States. McDonald's has restaurants in more than 115 nations. Since 1986, *The Economist* magazine has used "The Big Mac Index," showing the cost of a Big Mac in cities around the world, as a way to compare the value of different currencies.

McDonald's has become an institution not only in the United States but also around the world. When the Kuwait City McDonald's opened in 1994, the line for the drive-thru stretched for seven miles. More than 10,000 Russians waited in line for days to apply for jobs at Russia's first McDonald's when it opened its doors at the end of the cold war. For many of the world's urban poor, eating at McDonald's is a status symbol.

This global image has also stirred up anti-American and anti-globalization sentiment. McDonald's is often targeted by protesters who see it as a symbol of America's dominant cultural presence. Others fault McDonald's for popularizing junk food and for the environmental degradation they associate with the demand for beef generated by McDonald's and other fast-food restaurant chains. Meanwhile, customers continue to stop at McDonald's. The McDonald's-related issues addressed by protesters arise from ongoing consumer demand for McDonald's products.

Further Reading

Cohon, George, with David Macfarlane. *To Russia with Fries: My Adventures in Canada and Russia—Having Fun along the Way.* Toronto: McClelland & Stewart, 1997.

Kochan, Nicholas, ed. *The World's Greatest Brands.* New York: New York University Press, 1997.

Kroc, Ray, with Robert Anderson. *Grinding It Out: The Making of McDonald's.* New York: St. Martin's Paperbacks, 1987.

Love, John F. *McDonald's: Behind the Arches.* Rev. ed. New York: Bantam Books, 1995.

Pillsbury, Richard. *From Boarding House to Bistro: The American Restaurant Then and Now.* Boston: Unwin Hyman, 1990.

Watson, James L., ed. *Golden Arches East: McDonald's in East Asia.* Stanford, Calif.: Stanford University Press, 1997.

—Lisa Magloff

Mercantilism

Mercantilism was the prevailing economic philosophy from the emergence of the modern nation-state in the sixteenth century until the Industrial Revolution of the late eighteenth century. In the history of economic thought, it defines the period between the feudalism of the Middle Ages and the liberalism of the modern era. While feudalism was legitimized by theologians, and liberalism was theorized by philosophers, mercantilism was a government-developed economic system, created primarily through the practical policies of leaders of state.

Mercantilism comprises five chief features. First, mercantilism was founded on bullionism, the belief that a nation's wealth can be measured in terms of the amount of precious metals in its possession. Second, mercantilists held that the wealth of the nation was the responsibility of the government, which could discharge its bullionist duties in one of two ways: It could operate a favorable balance of trade (intervene to increase the nation's precious metal holdings by ensuring that the volume of exports exceeded the volume of imports), or it could acquire foreign territory as a source of gold and silver and raw materials, and as a guaranteed market for finished goods from the mother country. Third, mercantilism held that the world had a fixed amount of wealth and one nation could increase its share of that wealth only at the expense of other nations. Fourth, mercantilism maintained that national security demanded a high degree of economic self-sufficiency, the achievement of which required that trade be restricted as far as possible to exchanges between the nation and its colonies. Fifth, mercantilism contended that domestic economic competition would weaken a nation's economy in relation to the economies of its foreign competitors.

Historical Development

Mercantilism was the ideology of the merchants who rose to preeminent political influence in the newly consolidated nation-states

See also:
Capitalism; Hamilton, Alexander; Smith, Adam; Trade Policy; *Wealth of Nations, The.*

Mercantilism Time Line

1492
Columbus reaches the Americas.

1558 to 1603
The reign of Elizabeth I. Elizabeth encourages explorers such as John Hawkins and Francis Drake.

1661 to 1683
Jean-Baptiste Colbert serves as finance minister to Louis XIV, king of France.

1664
Thomas Mun publishes *England's Treasure by Foreign Trade.*

1720s
Unrealistic expectations inflate the South Sea Company's stock, leading to its collapse.

1754 to 1763
The French and Indian War.

1776
Adam Smith's *The Wealth of Nations* mounts a fierce philosophical challenge to mercantilism.

1776 to 1783
The Revolutionary War.

of Europe at the end of the Middle Ages. The power of this mercantile class was greatly enhanced by the economic opportunities afforded by the European discovery and exploitation of the Americas. In the mercantilist era, the leading monopoly corporations became the principal instruments of colonial policy for the leading European states and their recently acquired empires.

Under the leadership of Warren Hastings, the English East India Company emerged as a political rival of the imperial government, leading to Hastings's impeachment trial beginning in 1788. The growth of monopoly companies also marked the origin of the modern financial scandal, for example, the South Sea Bubble of the early 1720s, when unrealistic expectations inflated the value of stock in the South Sea Company, which subsequently collapsed. The mercantilist era was also one of commercial warfare, as nations fought over the limited supply of captive markets. Mercantilism was both a cause and an effect of these wars.

Spanish Mercantilism

The Spanish state came into existence with the marriage of King Ferdinand of Aragon and Queen Isabella of Castile in 1469. With its internal territories consolidated, the Spanish Crown financed a series of exploratory voyages that culminated in Columbus's arrival in the Americas in 1492 and the subsequent invasion by conquistadores such as Hernando Cortés and Francisco Pizarro. Its American empire supplied Spain with an abundance of gold and silver obtained not through the plundering of Aztec and Inca treasure, as is popularly supposed, but through the forced labor of native peoples in mines. African slaves were also imported to the Americas for the same purpose.

Trade relations between Spain and its American possessions were subject to the strictest mercantilist regulation. Only Spanish shipping could carry goods between Spain and the Americas; to facilitate government regulation, all colonial trade was channeled through only a few designated Spanish ports. To fully integrate the colonial economy with the Spanish national economy, the Crown prohibited the development of manufacturing in its territories, thus keeping those territories as markets for Spanish manufactured goods.

French Mercantilism

In France, mercantilism has its origins in the regulatory practices of Jean-Baptiste Colbert, finance minister to Louis XIV from 1661 to 1683. Colbert saw commercial expansion as a prerequisite for effective state power. Consequently, he created monopoly charter companies and directed French capital into export industries and into import-substitution projects.

At the same time, the French economy was insulated with protective tariffs, and foreign corporations were excluded from trade within the French empire. All of the above was achieved without significant reform of the domestic economy, which remained substantially feudal. The resultant economic stagnation would make France fertile territory for anti-mercantilist ideas in the eighteenth century.

British Mercantilism

Britain began its long mercantilist experiment in the reign of Elizabeth I (1558–1603). Elizabeth rewarded enterprise by granting monopoly privileges to distinguished merchants. At the same time, English seamen, including John Hawkins and Francis Drake, mounted a naval challenge to Spanish trade routes between Europe and the Americas.

British mercantilism developed further with a series of Navigation Acts in the seventeenth century; these laws required that imports from British colonies in Asia, Africa,

---

Mercantilism: Key Ideas

✔ A nation's wealth depends on the possession of precious metals.
✔ National security demands economic self-sufficiency.
✔ Government must exercise strong control of industry and trade.
✔ A nation grows wealthier only at the expense of other nations.
✔ Exports are more important than imports or domestic trade.

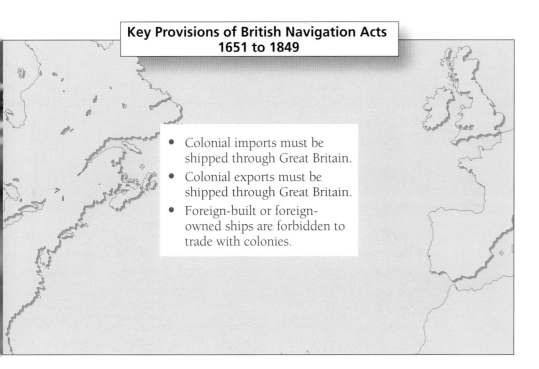

**Key Provisions of British Navigation Acts
1651 to 1849**

- Colonial imports must be shipped through Great Britain.
- Colonial exports must be shipped through Great Britain.
- Foreign-built or foreign-owned ships are forbidden to trade with colonies.

and North America be carried only in British ships. These acts led to several wars between the British and the Dutch in the second half of the seventeenth century.

Assaults on Mercantilism

The effect of mercantilism was to politicize trade, with the result that trade disputes rapidly escalated into political conflicts, the most spectacular example being the Revolutionary War (1776–1783). Faced with serious public debt at the end of the French and Indian War (1754–1763), the British sought to transfer a greater share of North American defense costs to the colonists. The London government therefore imposed a variety of revenue-raising measures in the 13 colonies, including the Sugar Act of 1764, the Stamp Act of 1765, and the Townsend Acts of 1767. These met with severe resistance from the colonists.

Without doubt, much of this resistance stemmed from constitutional and philosophical objections to taxation without representation. Clearly the subsequent rebellion was also fueled by the economic costs imposed on the colonies by mercantilism. The Sugar Act, for example, forced colonists to buy sugar and molasses from the British West Indies, even though they were available more cheaply from the French Caribbean.

In 1776, the same year that Jefferson issued the Declaration of Independence, the Scottish philosopher Adam Smith (1723–1790) published *The Wealth of Nations*, which is widely taken to be the foundation text of modern economics. Smith developed a theory of wealth creation that was radically at variance with mercantilism. According to Smith, mercantilism was an ideology in the service of both the state and the more powerful vested interests within it.

Smith proposed an alternative economic philosophy, the object of which was to benefit the needs of consumers in general through economic growth. Such growth, he argued, was best achieved through the twin mechanisms of free market competition and the division of labor. Working from Smith's analysis, later liberal political economists, like David Ricardo (1772–1823), argued that international trade enabled countries to concentrate on economic activities in which they enjoyed a comparative advantage. Therefore, trade relations were potentially beneficial to all participants.

Mercantilism's few theoretical defenses, including Thomas Mun's *England's Treasure by Foreign Trade* (1664), could not withstand the force of the new liberal arguments. However, economic systems collapse because of practical, rather than theoretical, deficiencies. The

The signing of the Declaration of Independence in 1776; this, along with Adam Smith's The Wealth of Nations, *spelled the beginning of the end for mercantilism.*

mercantilist system was dismantled because its core assumptions were undermined by changing economic reality, especially by industrialization and the increased opportunities it created for specialization and the exploitation of comparative advantage.

Mercantilism in the Liberal Era

Paradoxically, mercantilism's most adept theoreticians emerged after its decline and its replacement with liberal economics. Alexander Hamilton (1757–1804) in the United States and Friedrich List (1789–1846) in Germany both advocated systems of protective tariffs behind which their young countries could industrialize and challenge the economic predominance of the British.

In the twentieth century, many developing countries experimented with mercantilist policies of national economic development, including the strategy of import-substitution industrialization pursued by the Institutional Party of the Revolution in Mexico after 1929. In advanced industrialized countries, powerful economic interest groups have continued to lobby for mercantilist protective tariffs or subsidies. Although mercantilism retreated in face of globalization in the late twentieth century, mercantilist ideas are still influential in popular economic debate, a prominent example being the notion that a positive balance of trade is always desirable.

Further Reading

Galbraith, John Kenneth. *A History of Economics.* London: H. Hamilton, 1987.
Heilbroner, Robert. *The Worldly Philosophers.* 7th ed. New York: Simon & Schuster, 1999.

—*Peter C. Grosvenor*

Merger and Acquisition

When two companies merge, they combine their assets as well as their liabilities; an acquiring company purchases the assets and assumes the liabilities of a "target" company, and the target company is merged into the acquiring company. An acquisition also involves an acquiring company purchasing the assets and assuming the liabilities of a target company. In the case of an acquisition, however, the target company technically remains in existence: it is still legally a company and owned by its former shareholders. Acquisitions are often treated as de facto mergers because the target company is usually dissolved and the payment received for its assets is distributed to its shareholders.

Although these definitions may sound relatively simple, successful completion of a merger or acquisition is a complex process, requiring a gamble on the part of both companies involved. Key players during a merger or acquisition include the boards of directors, who must keep the best interests of their stockholders in mind; accountants and professional investment advisers who determine the fairness of the exchange and weigh the benefits and risks; and attorneys who ensure the legality of the transaction. In the United States, the merger or acquisition may have to be approved by federal or state regulatory agencies and the Justice Department, which enforces compliance with U.S. antitrust regulations. It may also be necessary for the merging companies to file with the Securities and Exchange Commission (SEC), which oversees all public market stock transactions

The 1990s was characterized by unprecedented merger and acquisition activity, motivated by a combination of forces including globalization, technological advances, industry consolidation, and governmental deregulation. In 2001, even as the economy slumped and companies proceeded more cautiously, these forces continued to outweigh the risks involved in successfully completing and managing a merger. Indeed, 2001 saw the biggest merger in history with the combination of America Online (AOL) and Time-Warner, a deal valued at $183 billion.

The Benefits and Risks of Mergers and Acquisitions

Bigger is better, some say. This idea may seem to describe the primary motivation for companies to combine with one another, but usually the reasons for a merger or acquisition are more complicated and numerous. An acquiring company may want to eliminate competition for its products or services, or it might want to expand operations to areas where it currently has no presence and the target company does.

A merger or acquisition may also substantially increase operating efficiency. Similar operations can be combined to create synergy, which reduces costs even as output remains the same or rises. A merger may allow a company to manufacture new but closely related products, acquire broader consumer bases, or gain control of

See also:
Economic Growth;
Globalization; Multinational
Corporation; Regulation of
Business and Industry.

White and Not-So-White Knights

The language used in business and industry is rich with metaphor, allowing businesspeople to quickly express complex ideas in whirlwind sessions of deal making and breaking. Animal metaphors like "bear hug" describe a bidder's public offer to purchase the target company in an attempt to pressure, or squeeze, the target company into accepting. The "macaroni defense" involves issuing bonds whose value expands, like cooked pasta, in the event of an unwanted takeover. Video games have even found their way into the vernacular: "Pacman defense" describes a target company's attempt to take over the hostile bidder.

Some of the most common metaphors used in mergers and acquisitions are the "knight" metaphors used to describe the various companies involved in a hostile takeover. The "black knight" is the hostile acquiring company, whose bid is undesirable to the target company's board—often because the board consists of members of the management team who wish to retain their positions after the merger.

As part of a defense strategy, the board may seek out a "white knight," or favored bidder, to take over the company instead. A "gray knight" may also enter the picture. The gray knight is a second, unsolicited company that outbids a white knight in pursuit of its own interests. This outcome is less preferable to the target company than acquisition by the white knight but is still preferable to the black knight's hostile takeover.

suppliers. A car company, for instance, may find acquiring a steel company to be advantageous, as it would control both the cost and production of its supplies. The 2001 marriage of AOL and Time-Warner appeared to make sense for both companies: Time-Warner benefited from AOL's Internet distribution capabilities and large consumer base, while AOL benefited from Time-Warner's vast array of popular media content, which AOL lacked.

In the increasingly competitive global market, companies often decide that the easiest and quickest way to expand is by combining. Although other options for expansion exist—building new firms or factories from the ground up—companies that choose such options may find themselves easily outpaced by merging companies. Moreover, merger and acquisition activity necessarily creates more of the

same—more merger and acquisition activity. After the combination of AOL and Time-Warner, for instance, other media and Internet companies scrambled to combine to compete more effectively with the new media giant.

Although the benefits of a merger or acquisition are clear, any such deal is accompanied by risks to both parties: experts estimate that more than half of all mergers are not as successful as projected. A post-merger company may not achieve the expected savings or growth because of hidden costs, unforeseen operational incompatibilities, or the loss of critical staff. In other cases, forces like war or recession affect the economy and stock market, and the post-merger company does not earn as much as it had projected.

In an atmosphere of increased antitrust vigilance by the Justice Department, mergers may be judged anticompetitive, in which case companies may have to give up some interests to be permitted to combine. Exxon and Mobil, for instance, were forced to sell many service stations in the Northeast and other assets to get approval for their 1999 merger.

Sometimes the risks are to the merger itself rather than the post-merger corporation: the government may completely block a merger because of antitrust considerations. In the global market, organizations outside the United States are increasingly playing such a watchdog role. In 2001, for instance, the European Union effectively blocked a merger between GE and Honeywell because of antitrust concerns.

Finally, because a merger or acquisition offer can eliminate hundreds or even thousands of jobs, a bid may so alarm employees of the target corporation that, through protests and union pressure, they may successfully persuade government agencies to block the transaction.

Currency and Structural Options
The currency used in mergers and acquisitions is typically either cash or stock. In a cash merger, shareholders of the target

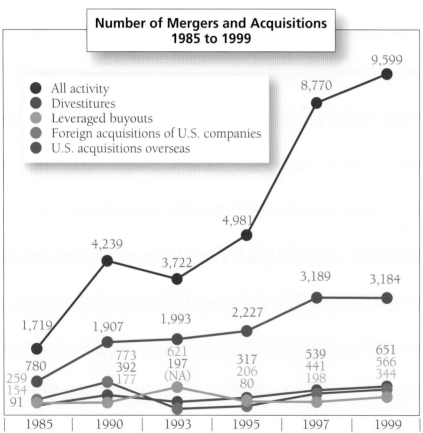

Number of Mergers and Acquisitions 1985 to 1999

- All activity
- Divestitures
- Leveraged buyouts
- Foreign acquisitions of U.S. companies
- U.S. acquisitions overseas

NA = Not available.

Notes: Covers transactions valued at $5 million or more. *All activity* includes mergers, acquisitions, acquisitions of partial interest that involve a 40 percent stake in the target or an investment of at least $100 million, divestitures, and leveraged transactions that result in a change in ownership. *Divestiture:* sale of a business, division, or subsidiary by a corporate owner. *Leveraged buyout:* acquisition of a business in which buyers use mostly borrowed money to finance purchase price.
Source: U.S. Bureau of the Census, *Statistical Abstract of the United States: 2001,* Washington, D.C., Government Printing Office, 2002.

company are paid cash for their stock in the company. In a stock merger, shareholders surrender the stock they own in the target company and receive stock of the acquiring company. Here, the target company must predict the value of the post-merger company's shares and project the stability and growth of the stock market itself. In a bull market (a market in which share values are rising), companies often find offering shares to be relatively cheap, but this exchange may lead to more of a gamble for the directors of the target company, who have an obligation to act in the shareholders' best interests.

Many structural options exist for a merger, but the three most common are direct merger, forward triangular merger, and reverse triangular merger. In a direct merger, two companies combine, with the target company disappearing into the acquiring company. The boards of directors and shareholders of the two companies must approve the merger/acquisition agreement. Although the management of the target company is typically replaced in such a merger, companies that are high profile and relatively equal may find combining both name and management, as in the case of the AOL Time-Warner merger, to be more valuable.

A direct merger may be the most efficient option when an acquiring company is satisfied that it has identified all of the liabilities of the target company. Sometimes, however, an acquiring company may be concerned about exposing itself to hidden or unknown liabilities of the target company, in which case it may choose a forward triangular or reverse triangular merger.

A forward triangular merger is a variation on the direct merger. Here, a wholly owned subsidiary, or secondary company, of the acquirer is merged into the target company, so that the target company is the surviving corporation and the subsidiary ceases to exist. The target company then becomes a wholly owned subsidiary of the acquiring company. All of the target company's liabilities are still

its own; no claim can be made against the central assets of the acquiring company.

In a reverse triangular merger, the target company merges into a wholly owned subsidiary of the acquirer. The subsidiary acquires all of the target's assets and assumes all of its liabilities. As in the previous option, the acquiring company does not expose itself to hidden or unforeseen liabilities.

Strategic Considerations and Hostile Takeovers

In a merger with cash used as the currency of exchange, the transaction is fairly straightforward. In a stock exchange merger, however, the target company's board must carefully consider to what extent the deal will benefit shareholders. If more than one bidder makes an offer, the board's decision must be based not on the immediate value of the

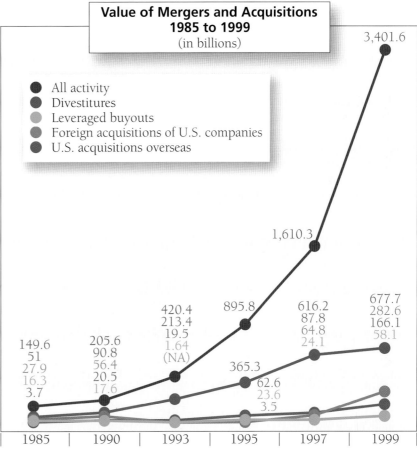

Value of Mergers and Acquisitions 1985 to 1999
(in billions)

- All activity
- Divestitures
- Leveraged buyouts
- Foreign acquisitions of U.S. companies
- U.S. acquisitions overseas

NA = Not available.
Notes: Covers transactions valued at $5 million or more. *All activity* includes mergers, acquisitions, acquisitions of partial interest that involve a 40 percent stake in the target or an investment of at least $100 million, divestitures, and leveraged transactions that result in a change in ownership. *Divestiture:* sale of a business, division, or subsidiary by a corporate owner. *Leveraged buyout:* acquisition of a business in which buyers use mostly borrowed money to finance purchase price.
Source: U.S. Bureau of the Census, *Statistical Abstract of the United States: 2001*, Washington, D.C., Government Printing Office, 2002.

bid but on the transaction that offers the best long-term prospects for growth and value enhancement. Will the merger increase the competitive presence of the company? Will it lower costs, and is there the potential for synergy? How do the bidder's experience and opportunities compare with those of others?

If a target company's directors do not want to accept the terms of the bid, the merger may turn into a hostile takeover. As a defensive tactic, the target company may seek another, favored bidder (commonly referred to as a "white knight") with whom to broker a deal. If the target company's board includes members of its management team, they may experience a conflict of interest. A white knight's offer might be less lucrative, but it also might come with the understanding that management would not be replaced or would find equivalent jobs in the combined company. If shareholders were able to prove some directors acted out of their own interest, they might have reason to sue. Because directors are expected to make choices based on long-term benefits, however, they have a substantial range

for the exercise of their business judgment, and they are protected in the courts by the business judgment rule, which burdens plaintiffs with proving that directors' decisions were not made in the best interests of the corporation.

In defending against hostile takeovers, target companies may also choose to sell a desirable part of the business, thus eliminating the reason for the takeover. They may opt to buy new businesses or properties that create antitrust or regulatory problems for the bidder. These tactics, known as "scorched earth defenses," make the target less attractive to the acquirer.

The acquiring company has strategic considerations as well. Prior to offering a merger, the acquiring company must exercise due diligence: it must research the target company to evaluate the benefits and risks of a merger, using resources like SEC filings, operating budgets, reports from consultants, and previous acquisition agreements. A key goal of due diligence is the uncovering of undervalued, overvalued, and unrecorded assets and liabilities. In a hostile takeover, the difficulties of due diligence are magnified because the target company often refuses to cooperate in providing information.

When attempting a hostile takeover, the acquiring company may start a proxy contest, which is a way to take control of a company without owning the majority of its voting stock. In its simplest form, a proxy contest occurs when a group of "dissident" shareholders (typically a noncontrolling group) tries to persuade other shareholders to elect a new slate of directors who will vote in favor of the merger.

The Future of Mergers and Acquisitions

Merger and acquisition activity is a product of economic growth and globalization. The United States has always led the world in merger and acquisition deals, but overseas corporations are fast closing the gap: in 1999 the number of overseas deals, if not the dollar amount, exceeded deals made by U.S. companies for the first time.

Michael Eisner (left), chairman and CEO of the Walt Disney Company, talks with Mel Woods (right), president and CEO of Haim Saban, during announcement of purchase by Disney of Fox Family Worldwide and Haim Saban in July 2001. Projected behind them are the logos of the new acquisitions.

Our Community. Our Bank.

In the United States, the number of completed deals dropped after a decade of unprecedented increase, but the net value of those deals climbed to a record high. As companies seek to expand their global networks in an increasingly connected world, this upward spiral will most likely continue, though the impact of the economic recession that began in 2001 is yet to be fully measured.

Mergers and acquisitions create bigger businesses, which in turn create more mergers and acquisitions, which result in multinational companies that have a unique ability to increase national and individual wealth, provide necessary and useful products, and forge friendships between nations. At the same time, the influence and interests of such large corporations draw criticism from groups that note, among other problems, environmental abuses, violations of workers' and children's rights, and undue corporate influence on government policy. As globalization stimulates merger and acquisition activity and vice versa, close monitoring will be necessary so that the advantages of such activity are not counterbalanced by costs to human rights and the environment.

Further Reading

Miller, Brian J., ed. *Mergers and Acquisitions.* New York: John Wiley and Sons, 1994.

Sikora, Martin. "The Panorama of Mergers and Acquisitions." *Mergers and Acquisitions,* 4 April 2000.

Wasserstein, Bruce. *Big Deal: Mergers and Acquisitions in the Digital Age.* New York: Warner Books, 1998.

Weston, J. Fred, and Samuel C. Weaver. *Mergers and Acquisitions.* New York: McGraw-Hill, 2001.

—*John Troyer and Andrea Troyer*

In 2001 a merger of several banks created the Boston Bank of Commerce, the first African American–owned national bank. Basketball star Earvin "Magic" Johnson, left, and music executive Jheryl Busby, second from left, are shareholders.

Merger and Acquisition   857

Merrill Lynch

More than any other brokerage firm, Merrill Lynch is responsible for making the stock market accessible to the average American. During the first part of the twentieth century, anyone who did not work for a brokerage had great difficulty getting information about the markets. In 1940, the year Charles Edward Merrill founded the firm now known as Merrill Lynch & Company, less than 10 percent of American households invested in the financial markets. Sixty years later, more than 60 percent of American households have investments, and mutual funds alone hold more of America's financial assets than banks.

Merrill was born in Green Cove Springs, Florida, in 1885, the son of a country physician. Merrill attended Amherst College for two years but was forced to drop out because of lack of funds. He talked his way into a job at the New York firm of George H. Burr & Company, and in a short time was head of the company's new bonds department. While there, he struck up a friendship with Edmund C. Lynch, who was selling soda fountain equipment. In 1914 the two men opened a brokerage firm called Charles E. Merrill and Company (16 months later the name was changed to Merrill, Lynch & Company). This firm made its name underwriting fledgling retail chain stores like McCrory, Kresges (now K-Mart), and Safeway. Merrill, Lynch & Company also became famous as the first brokerage to hire a bond saleswoman (Annie Grimes, in 1919).

Merrill became famous for the frequency with which he appeared in the gossip columns. By 1940 he had been married three times and had three children; the youngest, James Merrill, became one of America's leading poets. The elder Merrill's flamboyant behavior gave rise to the expression "Good Time Charlie."

As the Roaring '20s came to a close, Merrill was one of the few people in Wall Street to realize that the dizzy spiral of speculation could not last much longer. In the months leading up to the 1929 Wall Street crash, Merrill pleaded with President Calvin Coolidge to speak out against speculation and align himself with more conservative Wall Street forces. The firm mailed out a letter urging customers to get out of debt and out of the market.

By February 1929 Merrill was so sure the end was near that he liquidated the firm's stock portfolio, an act that left Merrill Lynch one of the few brokerages still standing after October 29, 1929. At the time of the stock market crash, Merrill's foresight was estimated to have saved more than $6 million for the firm's customers. Of this

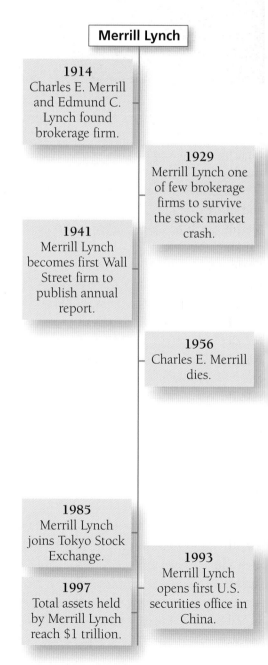

Merrill Lynch

1914 Charles E. Merrill and Edmund C. Lynch found brokerage firm.

1929 Merrill Lynch one of few brokerage firms to survive the stock market crash.

1941 Merrill Lynch becomes first Wall Street firm to publish annual report.

1956 Charles E. Merrill dies.

1985 Merrill Lynch joins Tokyo Stock Exchange.

1993 Merrill Lynch opens first U.S. securities office in China.

1997 Total assets held by Merrill Lynch reach $1 trillion.

The pneumatic tube center at the New York office of Merrill Lynch in 1955. Messages originating in various departments were put in these tubes to be wired to offices all over the country.

foresight, Merrill once said, "The lesson that I had learned—when stocks are too high they come down—stood me in good stead in 1928–29."

In 1930 Merrill sold the retail brokerage end of his company to E.A. Pierce, leaving Merrill Lynch to concentrate on investment banking. This firm also founded *Family Circle* magazine as a sideline. *Family Circle* was the first grocery store point-of-sale publication and a runaway success.

Merrill saw that the crash of 1929 and the Depression that followed had destroyed America's faith in the stock market. Merrill and his partners believed that the way to rebuild that faith was by rebuilding the market using the small investor as a foundation. In 1940 Merrill Lynch rejoined E.A. Pierce (then E.A. Pierce & Cassatt) to form Merrill Lynch & Company This company became the vehicle for Merrill's vision to "bring Wall Street to Main Street."

For average people to invest in the market, they first had to understand it. In the 1940s no books or pamphlets describing the market in lay terms were available. To convince people to invest, Merrill Lynch published an endless stream of reports, magazines, and pamphlets with titles like

"What Everyone Ought to Know about This Stock and Bond Business." Merrill Lynch became the first Wall Street firm to publish an annual report (1941) and the first to establish a training school for account executives. The firm gave seminars across the country, providing child care so that both husband and wife could attend. It set up tents at county fairs and ran a brokerage on wheels to reach rural customers. These efforts helped make Merrill Lynch the largest brokerage in the country. By Merrill's death in 1956, the firm had some 400,000 clients.

Although the United States had not been transformed into a nation of investors by 1956, Merrill Lynch had set a precedent that other firms would follow. Over the

> Now is the time to get out of debt. We think you should know that with a few exceptions all the larger companies financed by us today have no funded debt. This is not the result of luck but of carefully considered plans on the part of their managements and ourselves to place these companies in an impregnable position. The advice that we have given important corporations can be followed to advantage by all classes of investors. We do not urge you to sell securities indiscriminately, but we advise you in no uncertain terms that you take advantage of present high prices and put your own financial house in order. We recommend that you sell enough securities to lighten your obligations, or better yet, pay them entirely.
>
> —Charles Merrill's 1928 letter to his investors

The Jersey City, New Jersey, offices of Merrill Lynch in 2001.

next 40 years Merrill Lynch, along with many other brokerage firms, continued to push Wall Street and Main Street closer together by making Wall Street accessible to the small investor. The basics first taught by Merrill Lynch have become common knowledge: People should invest for the long term; they should understand the companies they are buying; and despite its ups and downs, the market is one of the safest forms of investment.

Merrill Lynch was also one of the first companies to realize the importance of the emerging Asian equities markets, establishing a Hong Kong office in 1982, becoming the first foreign securities firm to be a regular member of the Tokyo Stock Exchange in 1985, and opening the first U.S. securities office in China in 1993. During the bull market (period of rising prices) of the 1980s and 1990s, Merrill Lynch was in the forefront of the move to get the individual investor more involved in the market; to that end Merrill Lynch was the first investment firm to issue securities online and bring investing into people's living rooms. By 1995 Merrill Lynch had become the largest equity organization in the world, and in 1997 the company's total assets in private client accounts had reached $1 trillion.

Merrill Lynch's reputation was damaged in 2002, when an investigation by Eliot Spitzer, the attorney general of New York state, revealed that investors had lost money because of what Spitzer described as "excessively bullish" stock recommendations from Merrill Lynch analysts. E-mails were disclosed in which analysts privately scoffed at particular stocks that were listed as official Merrill Lynch recommendations. Although Merrill Lynch admitted to no wrongdoing, the company agreed to pay $100 million to New York and other states and initiated structural changes aimed at keeping stock analysis independent from the company's own financial interests.

By building America's faith in the stock market, Merrill Lynch helped turn luxuries of the 1920s, including retirement and college funds, into the basic expectations of the American middle class. In light of the scandals and stock market decline of 2002, that faith appears to need restoring.

Further Reading

Nocera, Joseph. *A Piece of the Action: How the Middle Class Joined the Money Class.* New York: Simon & Schuster, 1994.

Stiles, Paul. *Riding the Bull: My Year in the Madness at Merrill Lynch.* New York: Times Business/Random House, 1998.

—Lisa Magloff

Glossary

arbitration Method of resolving disputes by use of a neutral third party to hear arguments and make a ruling. See encyclopedia entry.

bar code Series of vertical lines (bars) that represent a universal inventory number assigned to a given product. See encyclopedia entry.

bond A certificate stating that a firm or government will pay the holder regular interest payments and a set sum upon a specific maturity date.

brokerage Business that sells investment vehicles and advice. See encyclopedia entry, Security Industry.

capital Money or wealth that is put at risk to fund a business enterprise. See encyclopedia entry.

cartel Group of producers in an industry that band together to coordinate output and prices, sometimes with government support. See encyclopedia entry.

coincident index A measure of current economic activity.

communism Economic and social system based on group ownership of the means of production; goods and services are allocated by the central government. See encyclopedia entry.

comparative advantage One nation's ability to produce a good at a lower opportunity cost than can another nation. See encyclopedia entry.

copyright The exclusive ownership rights of authors, artists, or corporations to their works. See encyclopedia entry.

depression Recession of unusual length and severity. See encyclopedia entries, Great Depression, Recession.

development economics Study of how a society can achieve high productivity and better living standards.

e-commerce Conducting business transactions over the Internet.

equity (owner's equity) The amount invested in a business by the owners as well as the cumulative profits or losses from business operations.

equity (stock) A portion of ownership in a corporation. See encyclopedia entry, Stocks and Bonds.

feudalism System of government wherein rulers granted land to nobles in exchange for loyalty; the nobles then allowed peasants residency in return for taxes and labor.

fiscal policy Process of managing economic expansions and contractions by adjusting government spending to stabilize incomes and economic performance. See encyclopedia entry.

franchise License to operate a business that is part of a larger chain. See encyclopedia entry.

gross domestic product (GDP) Estimate of the value of goods and services produced within a country over a given period. See encyclopedia entry.

import substitution Encouraging economic development by limiting imports to encourage domestic production.

inflation Period of rising prices. See encyclopedia entry.

joint venture Two or more businesses cooperating to produce a good or service.

lagging index Measures of economic activity that change after the business cycle has turned.

liberalism In economics, the belief that a nation's wealth can achieve greatest increase through minimum government interference with trade.

limited liability Legal business structure whereby the business losses of owners are limited to their original investment. See encyclopedia entries, Liability, Partnership.

liquidity The ease with which assets can be converted into cash without a decline in value. See encyclopedia entry, Assets and Liabilities.

mass production Use of machines to produce goods in large numbers. See encyclopedia entry, Assembly Line.

mediation Method of dispute resolution in which a neutral third party hears the positions of both sides and assists them in reaching a settlement by offering expert opinion and suggestions. See encyclopedia entry, Arbitration.

monetary policy Government's use of its power over the money supply to influence economic growth and inflation. See encyclopedia entry.

money supply Amount of money in an economy.

monopoly Type of market that involves only one seller. See encyclopedia entry.

monopsony Market with a single buyer of a good or service.

pension Retirement savings plan offered through the employer.

portfolio Investments owned by a person or group.

productivity Amount of work that can be completed in a given time. See encyclopedia entry.

prototype Working model of a product. See encyclopedia entry, Patent.

recession Period in which overall economic output declines. See encyclopedia entry.

securities Stocks, bonds, and other financial instruments. See encyclopedia entry, Stocks and Bonds.

stagflation Condition of simultaneously rising unemployment and inflation.

subsidiary A business controlled by another business.

supply chain Series of businesses and transactions involved in producing a finished good or service.

tariff Tax on imported goods. See encyclopedia entry.

Index

Page numbers in **boldface** type indicate article titles. Page numbers in *italic* type indicate illustrations or other graphics.